Houghton
Mifflin
Harcourt

MATH Expressions
Common Core

Dr. Karen C. Fuson

GRADE

2

Volume 1

This material is based upon work supported by the
National Science Foundation
under Grant Numbers
ESI-9816320, REC-9806020, and RED-935373.

Any opinions, findings, and conclusions, or recommendations expressed in this material
are those of the author and do not necessarily reflect the views of the National Science Foundation.

VOLUME 1 CONTENTS

UNIT 1 Addition and Subtraction Within 20

BIG IDEA 1   Strategies for Addition and Subtraction

© Houghton Mifflin Harcourt Publishing Company

* This lesson consists only of activities from the Teacher Edition.

UNIT 2 Addition Within 200

© Houghton Mifflin Harcourt Publishing Company

© Houghton Mifflin Harcourt Publishing Company

* This lesson consists only of activities from the Teacher Edition.

UNIT 3 Length and Shapes

© Houghton Mifflin Harcourt Publishing Company

Family Letter

Dear Family:

Your child is learning math in a program called *Math Expressions,* which links mathematical ideas to a child's everyday experiences. This helps children understand math better.

In this program, your child will learn math and have fun by

- working with objects and making drawings of math situations.
- listening to and working with other children and sharing ways to solve problems.
- writing and solving problems and connecting math to daily life.
- helping classmates learn.

Your child will have homework almost every day. He or she needs a Homework Helper. The helper may be anyone—a family member, an older brother or sister, a neighbor, or a friend. Set aside a definite time for homework and provide your child with a quiet place to work where there are no distractions. Encourage your child to talk about what is happening in math class. If your child is having problems with math, please talk to me to see how you might help.

Please cut, fill in, and return the bottom part of this letter.

Thank you. You are very important to your child's learning.

Sincerely,
Your child's teacher

COMMON CORE Unit 1 includes the Common Core Standards for Mathematical Content for Operations and Algebraic Thinking 2.OA.1, 2.OA.2, 2.OA.3, Numbers and Operations in Base Ten 2.NBT.5, 2.NBT.6, 2.NBT.9, and all Mathematical Practices.

- -

My child _____ will have
(child's name)

_____ as a Homework Helper.
(name of homework helper)

This person is my child's _____.
(relationship to child)

_____
signature of parent or guardian

Estimada familia:

Su niño está aprendiendo matemáticas con un programa llamado *Math Expressions,* que relaciona conceptos matemáticos abstractos con la experiencia diaria de los niños. Esto ayuda a los niños a entender mejor las matemáticas.

Con este programa, su niño va a aprender matemáticas y se divertirá mientras:

- trabaja con objetos y hace dibujos de situaciones matemáticas.
- escucha y trabaja con otros estudiantes y comparte con ellos estrategias para resolver problemas.
- escribe y resuelve problemas, y relaciona las matemáticas con la vida diaria.
- ayuda a sus compañeros de clase a aprender.

Su niño tendrá tarea casi todos los días y necesitará que alguna persona lo ayude. Esa persona puede ser, usted, un hermano mayor, un vecino o un amigo. Establezca una hora para la tarea y ofrezca a su niño un lugar donde trabajar sin distracciones. Anímelo a comentar lo que está aprendiendo en la clase de matemáticas. Si él tiene problemas con las matemáticas, hable por favor con el maestro para ver cómo puede usted ayudar.

Por favor recorte, complete y devuelva el formulario al maestro.

Muchas gracias. Usted es imprescindible en el aprendizaje de su niño.

Atentamente,
El maestro de su niño

COMMON CORE La Unidad 1 incluye los Common Core Standards for Mathematical Content for Operations and Algebraic Thinking 2.OA.1, 2.OA.2, 2.OA.3, Numbers and Operations in Base Ten 2.NBT.5, 2.NBT.6, 2.NBT.9, and all Mathematical Practices.

- -

La persona que ayudará a mi niño _____ es
(nombre del niño)

_____. Esta persona es
(nombre de la persona)

_____ de mi niño.
(relación con el niño)

_____
Su firma

Name _____

► **Relate Math Mountains and Equations for Addition**

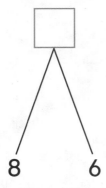

$8 + 6 = \boxed{}$

Discuss the **Math Mountain** and the **equation**.

1. Where is the **total**? Where are the **partners** or **addends**?

2. Tell word problems for both.

3. Solve both and compare your strategies.

► **Relate Math Mountains and Equations for Subtraction**

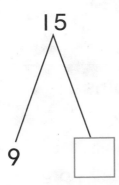

$9 + \boxed{} = 15$

$15 - 9 = \boxed{}$

Discuss this Math Mountain and the equations.

4. Where is the total? Where are the partners or addends?

5. Tell word problems for all.

6. Solve all and compare your strategies.

Name _____

► Count On for Addition or Subtraction

7. For addition, I pretend I already counted 9. Then
I count on 3 more to get the total. I stop when I
see/feel 3. I hear 12, the unknown total.

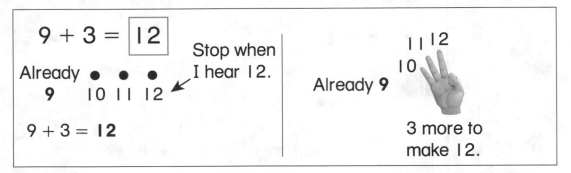

8. For subtraction, I pretend I already counted 9.
I count on until I get to 12. I stop when I hear 12.
I see/feel 3, the unknown partner.

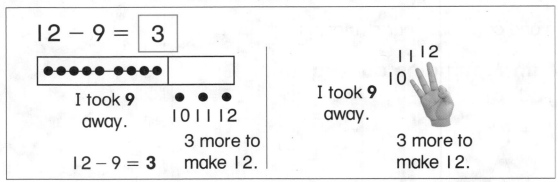

► Patterns in Equations for Math Mountains

9. Discuss patterns in the eight equations for the Math
Mountain with total 12 and partners 9 and 3.

$9 + 3 = 12$  $12 = 9 + 3$

$3 + 9 = 12$  $12 = 3 + 9$

$12 - 9 = 3$ $3 = 12 - 9$

$12 - 3 = 9$ $9 = 12 - 3$

Represent Addition and Subtraction

▶ Write Equations for Math Mountains

10. Write two equations for each Math Mountain.

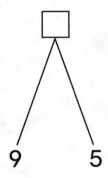

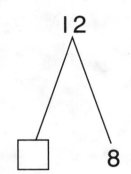

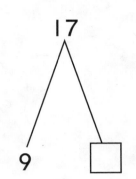

$9 + 5 = \square$

_____

_____

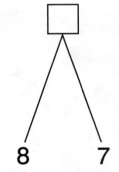

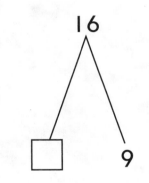

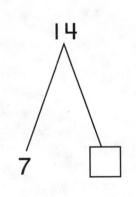

_____

_____

▶ Draw Math Mountains

11. Draw a Math Mountain and write one more equation.

$9 + 6 = \boxed{}$

_____

$9 + \boxed{} = 12$

_____

$8 + \boxed{} = 16$

_____

$5 + 6 = \boxed{}$

_____

$13 - 4 = \boxed{}$

_____

$15 - 7 = \boxed{}$

_____

Dear Family:

Your child is exploring addition and subtraction equations with Math Mountain Cards. The cards have a large number at the top and two smaller numbers at the bottom. From the cards, children can see that two smaller numbers can be added together to make a larger number. They can also see that a large number can be broken apart into two smaller numbers.

Children will write addition and subtraction equations that they can make from the cards, as shown in the example. The two partners, 9 and 6, can be added to make the total, 15. They can be switched (6 and 9) and still make 15.

$$9 + 6 = 15$$

$$6 + 9 = 15$$

$$15 - 9 = 6$$

$$15 - 6 = 9$$

15

$$9 + 6$$

$$15 = 9 + 6$$

$$15 = 6 + 9$$

$$6 = 15 - 9$$

$$9 = 15 - 6$$

Students see and write all eight equations. It is important for understanding algebra that they sometimes see equations with only one number on the left.

Please call if you need practice materials. Thank you for helping your child learn about the relationship between addition and subtraction.

Sincerely,
Your child's teacher

 COMMON CORE

Unit 1 includes the Common Core Standards for Mathematical Content for Operations and Algebraic Thinking 2.OA.1, 2.OA.2, 2.OA.3, Numbers and Operations in Base Ten 2.NBT.5, 2.NBT.6, 2.NBT.9, and all Mathematical Practices.

Estimada familia:

Su niño está aprendiendo ecuaciones de suma y resta usando las tarjetas *Math Mountain*. Las tarjetas tienen un número grande en la parte superior y dos números más pequeños en la parte inferior. En las tarjetas los niños pueden ver que se pueden sumar dos números más pequeños para obtener un número más grande. También pueden ver que un número grande se puede separar en dos números más pequeños.

Los niños escribirán ecuaciones de suma y resta que puedan hacer a partir de las tarjetas, según se muestra en el ejemplo. Se pueden sumar las dos partes, 9 y 6, para obtener el total, 15. También se pueden intercambiar (6 y 9) y todavía obtener 15.

$9 + 6 = 15$

$6 + 9 = 15$

$15 - 9 = 6$

$15 - 6 = 9$

$15 = 9 + 6$

$15 = 6 + 9$

$6 = 15 - 9$

$9 = 15 - 6$

Los estudiantes ven y escriben las ocho ecuaciones. Para comprender álgebra es importante que vean ecuaciones con un solo número a la izquierda.

Por favor comuníquese conmigo si necesita materiales para practicar. Gracias por ayudar a su niño a aprender la relación entre suma y resta.

Atentamente,
El maestro de su niño

COMMON CORE

La Unidad 1 incluye los Common Core Standards for Mathematical Content for Operations and Algebraic Thinking 2.OA.1, 2.OA.2, 2.OA.3, Numbers and Operations in Base Ten 2.NBT.5, 2.NBT.6, 2.NBT.9, and all Mathematical Practices.

Math Mountain Cards **9**

Math Mountain Cards

5 + 3   3 + 7   4 + 3   5 + 4
7   9   10   8

8   10   6

4 + 3   6 + 3   4 + 6   4 + 4
8   10   6

6 + 3   4 + 7   4 + 6   5 + 9
11   12   11

12   11   13   11

8 + 3   4 + 8   9 + 2
12   14   13   15

5 + 8   9 + 9   8 + 7   9 + 6

13   12   14

5 + 7   5 + 9   7 + 6   9 + 6
15   16   18

7 + 7   9 + 7   9 + 8

14   16   17

8 + 7   8 + 8   9 + 9

Math Mountain Cards

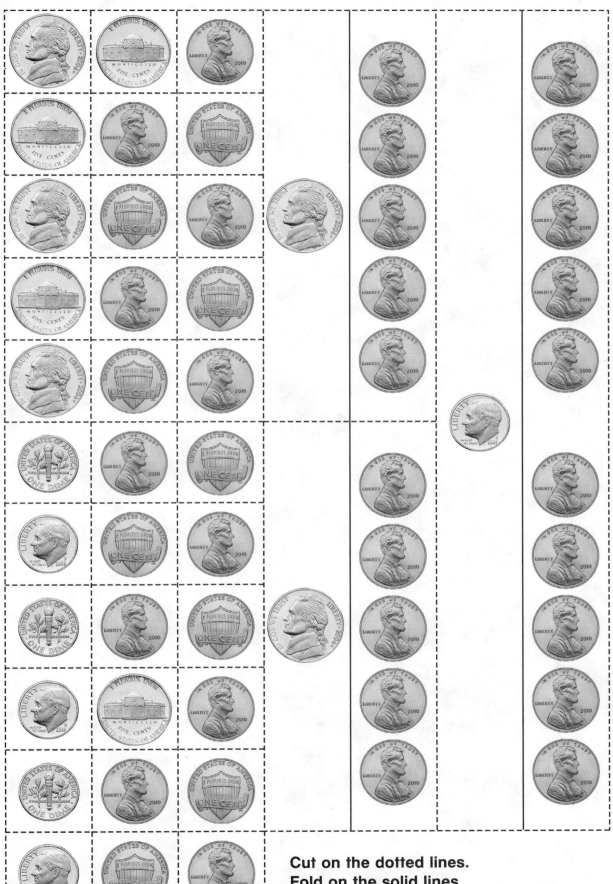

Cut on the dotted lines.
Fold on the solid lines.

Coin Strips **13**

Coin Strips

VOCABULARY
unknown addend

▶ Find the Unknown Addend

$$7 + \boxed{5} = 12$$

10
⌒
7 ● ● ● | ● ●

$$3 + 2 = 5$$

$$12 - 7 = \boxed{5}$$

● ● ● ● ● ● | ● ● ● | ● ●
7   5

Find the **unknown addend** (unknown partner).

1. $8 + \boxed{} = 11$ $15 - 6 = \boxed{}$ $8 + \boxed{} = 14$

2. $7 + \boxed{} = 13$ $12 - 8 = \boxed{}$ $3 + \boxed{} = 12$

3. $5 + \boxed{} = 14$ $16 - 9 = \boxed{}$ $9 + \boxed{} = 17$

4. $9 + \boxed{} = 14$ $18 - 9 = \boxed{}$ $7 + \boxed{} = 11$

5. $8 + \boxed{} = 13$ $13 - 9 = \boxed{}$ $15 - \boxed{} = 8$

13
╱╲
8   ☐

13
╱╲
9   ☐

15
╱╲
☐   8

6. Find the partner for $11 - 6 = \boxed{}$.

Make a math drawing to show what you did.

Name

▶ Practice Finding Teen Totals and Unknown Addends

Are we looking for a partner or total?
Ring the P or the T for each column.

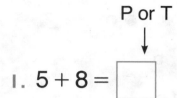

P or T P or T P or T

1. $5 + 8 = \square$ $7 + \square = 11$ $11 - 9 = \square$

2. $4 + 8 = \square$ $9 + \square = 17$ $16 - 8 = \square$

3. $7 + 9 = \square$ $7 + \square = 12$ $13 - 7 = \square$

4. $5 + 6 = \square$ $8 + \square = 16$ $14 - 7 = \square$

5. $7 + 6 = \square$ $9 + \square = 13$ $15 - 7 = \square$

6. $8 + 3 = \square$ $9 + \square = 18$ $14 - 9 = \square$

7. $8 + 4 = \square$ $6 + \square = 15$ $12 - 5 = \square$

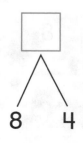

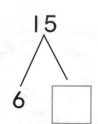

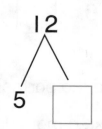

Relate Unknown Addends and Subtraction

VOCABULARY
pairs

► **Count by 2s**

1. Loop **pairs** of sleeping bags.

2. Number the sleeping bags from 1 to 50.

3. Count by 2s from 2 to 50.

2, ____, 6, ____, 10, ____, ____, 16, ____, ____,

____, 24, ____, ____, ____, ____, ____, 36, ____,

____, ____, ____, ____, ____, 50

VOCABULARY
pattern

▶ Patterns

Count by 2s to complete each **pattern**.

4. 6, 8, _____, _____, 14

5. 12, _____, _____, _____, 20

6. 26, _____, _____, _____, _____

7. _____, _____, _____, _____, 50

8. 50, _____, _____, _____, 58

9. 76, _____, _____, _____, _____

▶ What's the Error?

> 2, 4, 6, 8, 12, 14, 16, 18,
>
> 22, 24, 26, 28

I counted by 2s to 28. Did I count correctly?

10. Show how to count by 2s from 2 to 28.

2, _____, _____, _____, _____, _____, _____, _____, _____,

_____, _____, _____, _____, 28

VOCABULARY
odd
even

► **Make Pairs**

Draw lines to make pairs.

Ring **odd** or **even**.

11.

(odd)   even

12.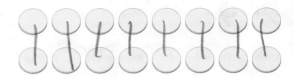

odd   (even)

13.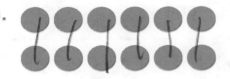

odd   (even)

14.

(odd)   even

15.

odd   (even)

16.

odd   (even)

17.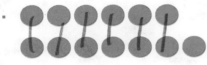

(odd)   even

18.

(odd)   even

19.

(odd)   even

20.

odd   (even)

VOCABULARY
addition doubles

► **Make Equal Groups**

Try to make equal groups.

Ring odd or even.

21. 9

odd   even

22. 6

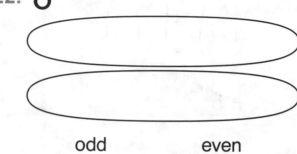

odd   even

23. 12

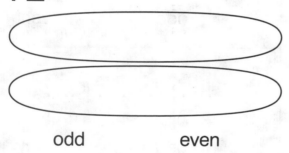

odd   even

24. 7

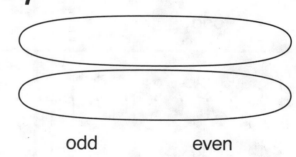

odd   even

► **Write Addition Doubles**

Complete the **addition doubles** equation.

25. ☐ + ☐ = 8

26. ☐ + ☐ = 10

27. ☐ + ☐ = 18

28. ☐ + ☐ = 16

Odd and Even Numbers

Name

▶ Use Doubles

Addition Doubles and **Subtraction Doubles**	**Doubles Plus 1** and **Doubles Minus 1**	**Doubles Plus 2** and **Doubles Minus 2**
1. $5 + 5 = \boxed{10}$	$5 + 6 = \boxed{11}$	$5 + 7 = \boxed{12}$
$10 - 5 = \boxed{5}$	$5 + 4 = \boxed{9}$	$5 + 3 = \boxed{8}$
2. $6 + 6 = \boxed{12}$	$6 + 7 = \boxed{13}$	$6 + 8 = \boxed{14}$
$12 - 6 = \boxed{6}$	$6 + 5 = \boxed{11}$	$6 + 4 = \boxed{10}$
3. $7 + 7 = \boxed{14}$	$7 + 8 = \boxed{15}$	$7 + 9 = \boxed{16}$
$14 - 7 = \boxed{7}$	$7 + 6 = \boxed{13}$	$7 + 5 = \boxed{12}$
4. $8 + 8 = \boxed{16}$	$8 + 9 = \boxed{17}$	$8 + 10 = \boxed{18}$
$16 - 8 = \boxed{8}$	$8 + 7 = \boxed{15}$	$8 + 6 = \boxed{14}$
5. $9 + 9 = \boxed{18}$	$9 + 10 = \boxed{19}$	$9 + 11 = \boxed{20}$
$18 - 9 = \boxed{9}$	$9 + 8 = \boxed{17}$	$9 + 7 = \boxed{16}$

Name _____

▶ Use Doubles (continued)

Add. Use doubles.

---

6. $9 + 9 = $ ☐ $8 + 6 = $ ☐ $6 + 5 = $ ☐

---

7. $7 + 7 = $ ☐ $7 + 6 = $ ☐ $9 + 11 = $ ☐

---

8. $11 + 9 = $ ☐ $6 + 8 = $ ☐ $6 + 6 = $ ☐

---

9. $7 + 9 = $ ☐ $5 + 5 = $ ☐ $8 + 7 = $ ☐

---

10. $9 + 8 = $ ☐ $5 + 7 = $ ☐ $6 + 4 = $ ☐

---

11. $8 + 8 = $ ☐ $8 + 10 = $ ☐ $9 + 7 = $ ☐

---

12. $5 + 4 = $ ☐ $6 + 7 = $ ☐ $5 + 6 = $ ☐

---

13. $7 + 8 = $ ☐ $8 + 9 = $ ☐ $7 + 5 = $ ☐

Strategies Using Doubles

VOCABULARY
equation
equation chain

▶ What's the Error?

1. Help Puzzled Penguin.

$$6 + 3 = \boxed{9} - 5$$

Did I make a mistake?

▶ Use Equations to Make an Equation Chain

2. Solve the **equations**.

   If the answer is 8, color the block  .

$8 + 9 = \Box$	$12 - 6 = \Box$	$7 + 5 = \Box$
$5 + 3 = \Box$	$17 - 9 = \Box$	$13 - 5 = \Box$
$5 + 4 = \Box$	$1 + 7 = \Box$	$15 - 8 = \Box$
$11 - 3 = \Box$	$4 + 4 = \Box$	$3 + 8 = \Box$
$16 - 8 = \Box$	$6 + 6 = \Box$	$5 + 7 = \Box$

3. Use the blocks you colored to make an **equation chain**.

_____

VOCABULARY
vertical form

► Show Three Ways

Write the equation, the **vertical form**, and the Math Mountain.

Use a ☐ to show the unknown number.

4. 8 and 5 make how many?

_____

5. 7 and what number make 15?

_____

6. 18 take away 8 equals what number?

_____

7. 17 minus 8 makes what number?

Dive the Deep

11 − 6 = 5 | 12 − 6 = 6 | 13 − 8 = 5

12 − 7 = 5 | 17 − 8 = 9 | 15 − 6 = 9

12 − 9 = 3 | 13 − 5 = 8 | 11 − 9 = 2

13 − 4 = 9 | 14 − 6 = 8 | 13 − 9 = 4

11 − 5 = 6 | 17 − 9 = 8 | 15 − 7 = 8

14 − 9 = 5 | 11 − 8 = 3 | 14 − 8 = 6

14 − 7 = 7 | 12 − 4 = 8 | 12 − 5 = 7

16 − 7 = 9 | 16 − 8 = 8 | 11 − 3 = 8

11 − 7 = 4 | 15 − 7 = 8 | 13 − 6 = 7

12 − 3 = 9 | 16 − 9 = 7 | 18 − 9 = 9

13 − 7 = 6 | 11 − 4 = 7 | 12 − 8 = 4

Dive the Deep

$11 - 5 = \boxed{6}$ $12 - \boxed{6} = 6$ $13 - 5 = \boxed{8}$

$12 - 5 = \boxed{7}$ $17 - \boxed{9} = 8$ $15 - 9 = \boxed{6}$

$12 - 3 = \boxed{9}$ $13 - \boxed{8} = 5$ $11 - 2 = \boxed{9}$

$13 - 9 = \boxed{4}$ $14 - \boxed{8} = 6$ $13 - 4 = \boxed{9}$

$11 - 6 = \boxed{5}$ $17 - \boxed{8} = 9$ $15 - 8 = \boxed{7}$

$14 - 5 = \boxed{9}$ $11 - \boxed{3} = 8$ $14 - 6 = \boxed{8}$

$14 - 7 = \boxed{7}$ $12 - \boxed{8} = 4$ $12 - 7 = \boxed{5}$

$16 - 9 = \boxed{7}$ $16 - \boxed{8} = 8$ $11 - 8 = \boxed{3}$

$11 - 4 = \boxed{7}$ $15 - \boxed{8} = 7$ $13 - 7 = \boxed{6}$

$12 - 9 = \boxed{3}$ $16 - \boxed{7} = 9$ $18 - 9 = \boxed{9}$

$13 - 6 = \boxed{7}$ $11 - \boxed{7} = 4$ $12 - 4 = \boxed{8}$

Dive the Deep

►Find a Sum of 10

Ring two addends that make ten. Then write the total.

1. $6 + 9 + 1 =$ ☐   2. $5 + 7 + 3 =$ ☐

3. $5 + 9 + 5 =$ ☐   4. $6 + 4 + 7 =$ ☐

5. $4 + 1 + 6 =$ ☐   6. $1 + 9 + 4 =$ ☐

7. $3 + 2 + 8 =$ ☐   8. $3 + 2 + 7 =$ ☐

►Add in Any Order

Write the total.

9. $9 + 3 + 5 =$ ☐   10. $9 + 7 + 2 =$ ☐

11. $8 + 9 + 2 =$ ☐   12. $7 + 8 + 5 =$ ☐

13. $7 + 5 + 2 =$ ☐   14. $7 + 7 + 2 =$ ☐

15. $3 + 9 + 6 =$ ☐   16. $3 + 8 + 2 =$ ☐

► **Add Four Addends**

Add in any order. Write the sum.

17. $4 + 4 + 5 + 2 =$ ☐   18. $8 + 8 + 5 + 2 =$ ☐

19. $5 + 5 + 3 + 9 =$ ☐   20. $3 + 6 + 5 + 4 =$ ☐

21. $4 + 8 + 9 + 3 =$ ☐   22. $1 + 8 + 8 + 4 =$ ☐

► ○ **PATH to FLUENCY** **Add and Subtract Within 20**

Add.

23. $6 + 8 =$ _____   24. $9 + 9 =$ _____   25. $7 + 0 =$ _____

26. $\begin{array}{r} 9 \\ +\ 7 \\ \hline \end{array}$ 27. $\begin{array}{r} 8 \\ +\ 5 \\ \hline \end{array}$ 28. $\begin{array}{r} 8 \\ +\ 2 \\ \hline \end{array}$ 29. $\begin{array}{r} 9 \\ +\ 9 \\ \hline \end{array}$

Subtract.

30. $\begin{array}{r} 15 \\ -\ 8 \\ \hline \end{array}$ 31. $\begin{array}{r} 9 \\ -\ 7 \\ \hline \end{array}$ 32. $\begin{array}{r} 9 \\ -\ 0 \\ \hline \end{array}$ 33. $\begin{array}{r} 12 \\ -\ 4 \\ \hline \end{array}$

Add Three or Four Addends

Dear Family:

Your child is learning to solve word problems called *Add To* and *Take From* problems. These problems begin with a quantity that is then modified by change—something is added or subtracted—which results in a new quantity.

Proof drawings show what your child was thinking when solving the problem. It is important that children label their drawings to link them to the problem situation.

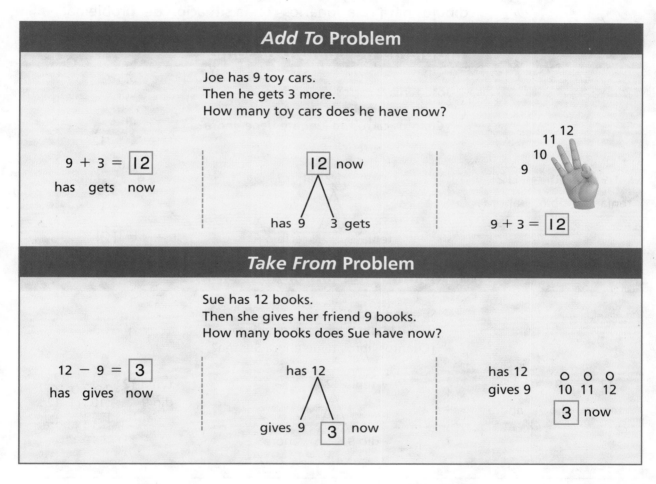

Please call if you have any questions or concerns.

Sincerely,
Your child's teacher

 COMMON CORE

Unit 1 includes the Common Core Standards for Mathematical Content for Operations and Algebraic Thinking 2.OA.1, 2.OA.2, 2.OA.3, Numbers and Operations in Base Ten 2.NBT.5, 2.NBT.6, 2.NBT.9, and all Mathematical Practices.

Carta a la familia

Estimada familia:

Su niño está aprendiendo a resolver problemas conocidos como problemas de *cambio al sumar* o de *cambio al restar*. Estos empiezan con una cantidad que luego es modificada por un cambio (algo que se suma o se resta), lo que resulta en una nueva cantidad.

Los dibujos muestran lo que su niño estaba pensando mientras resolvía el problema. Es importante que los niños rotulen sus dibujos para relacionarlos con la situación del problema.

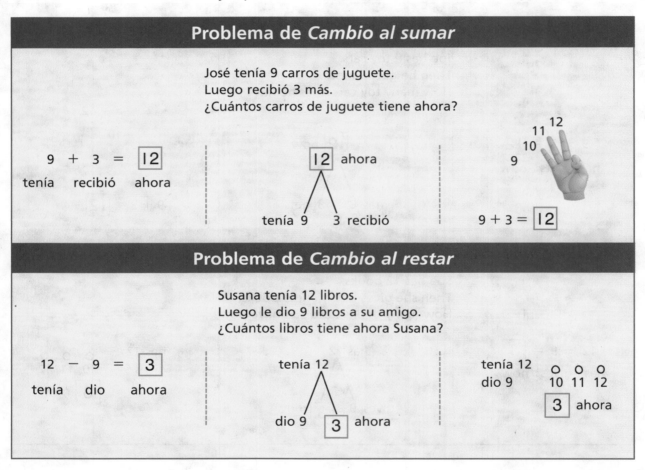

Problema de *Cambio al sumar*

José tenía 9 carros de juguete.
Luego recibió 3 más.
¿Cuántos carros de juguete tiene ahora?

$$9 + 3 = \boxed{12}$$
tenía recibió ahora

$\boxed{12}$ ahora

tenía 9   3 recibió

$9 + 3 = \boxed{12}$

Problema de *Cambio al restar*

Susana tenía 12 libros.
Luego le dio 9 libros a su amigo.
¿Cuántos libros tiene ahora Susana?

$$12 - 9 = \boxed{3}$$
tenía dio ahora

tenía 12

dio 9 $\boxed{3}$ ahora

tenía 12
dio 9

$\boxed{3}$ ahora

Si tiene alguna pregunta o algún comentario, por favor comuníquese conmigo.

Atentamente,
El maestro de su niño

© Houghton Mifflin Harcourt Publishing Company

COMMON CORE

La Unidad 1 incluye los Common Core Standards for Mathematical Content for Operations and Algebraic Thinking 2.OA.1, 2.OA.2, 2.OA.3, Numbers and Operations in Base Ten 2.NBT.5, 2.NBT.6, 2.NBT.9, and all Mathematical Practices.

Add To and *Take From* Word Problems

▶ **Solve and Discuss**

Make a drawing. Write an equation.
Solve the problem.

Show your work.

1. The school has 5 computers in
   the library. They buy some more
   computers. Now there are 12.
   How many computers does
   the school buy?

   school

   ☐ _____
          label

2. Alina has 17 beads. She uses 9 of
   them to make a bracelet. How many
   beads does she have left?

   beads

   ☐ _____
          label

3. Erin wraps 6 party favors. She needs
   to wrap 15 favors in all. How many
   favors does she still need to wrap?

   party favors

   ☐ _____
          label

► **Solve and Discuss (continued)**

Make a drawing. Write an equation.
Solve the problem.

Show your work.

children

4. There are 16 children at the playground.
Some children go home. Now there
are 7 children at the playground.
How many children went home?

☐ _____
    label

stamp

5. Lila has 6 stamps. Sam gives her
some more stamps. Now Lila has
14 stamps. How many stamps does
Sam give Lila?

☐ _____
    label

forest

6. There are 5 deer in the forest. 6 more
deer enter the forest. How many deer
are in the forest now?

☐ _____
    label

Add To and *Take From* Word Problems

▶ Solve and Discuss

Make a drawing. Write an equation.
Solve the problem.

Show your work.

1. Moshe has 5 toy cars. Mary gives him
   7 more toy cars. How many toy cars
   does Moshe have now?

   ☐ _____
        label

car

2. Heather buys 5 puzzles at a yard sale.
   Then her brother gives her some more.
   Now she has a total of 11 puzzles.
   How many puzzles did her brother
   give her?

   ☐ _____
        label

puzzle

3. The cook has 16 bags of potatoes.
   He uses some to make potato salad.
   Now he has 7 bags of potatoes left.
   How many bags did he use?

   ☐ _____
        label

potatoes

▶ Solve and Discuss (continued)

Make a drawing. Write an equation.
Solve the problem.

Show your work.

---

4. Charisa buys 4 new books. Now she has 13 books. How many books did Charisa have before?

book

☐ _____
         label

---

5. Shahla has 16 dolls. She gives 8 dolls to her sister. How many dolls does Shahla have now?

doll

☐ _____
         label

---

6. Brian has some tomato plants in his garden. 9 of the plants are eaten by bugs. 4 plants are left. How many plants did Brian have in the beginning?

bug

☐ _____
         label

Name _____

▶ Solve and Discuss

Make a drawing. Write an equation.
Solve the problem.

Show your work.

1. There are 13 people in a bike race. 8 are on top of the hill. The rest are at the bottom of the hill. How many people are at the bottom of the hill?

hill

☐ _____
label

2. 4 horses are in the barn. 8 horses are in the field. How many horses are on the farm altogether?

horse

☐ _____
label

3. Andrew makes some sandwiches. 6 are turkey sandwiches and 7 are ham sandwiches. How many sandwiches does Andrew make in all?

sandwich

☐ _____
label

4. Keisha has 11 cousins. 4 are boys and the rest are girls. How many are girls?

girl

☐ _____
label

▶ Solve and Discuss (continued)

Make a drawing. Write an equation. Solve the problem.

Show your work.

5. Latisha has 16 bags. 8 are small and the rest are large. How many large bags does Latisha have?

bag

[ ] _____
label

6. There are 7 books on the shelf and 5 on the table. How many books are there altogether?

book

[ ] _____
label

7. Mandy sews 8 blue beads and 6 red beads on a ribbon. How many beads are on the ribbon?

ribbon

[ ] _____
label

8. Lisa has 5 green pencils and some yellow pencils. She has 13 pencils in all. How many yellow pencils does Lisa have?

pencil

[ ] _____
label

Put Together/ Take Apart Problems

▶ Solve and Discuss

Make a drawing. Write an equation.
Solve the problem.

Show your work.

1. I have 12 flowers in a vase. 8 are daisies.
   The rest are roses. How many are roses?

   rose

   ☐ _____
   label

2. There are 13 animals at the animal shelter.
   7 of them are dogs. The rest are cats.
   How many cats are at the shelter?

   animal
   shelter

   ☐ _____
   label

3. Walt saw 4 crows. Then he saw some finches
   at the feeder. He saw 12 birds in all. How many
   finches were there?

   finch

   ☐ _____
   label

▶ You Decide

Complete this problem.

4. Jenna has 4 _____ and Bill

   has 6 _____. How many

   _____ do they have altogether?

   ☐ _____
   label

▶ Both Addends Unknown

5. Saira wants to put 7 flowers in a vase. She wants to use lilies and tulips. How many of each flower could she use?

☐ and ☐   7 = ☐ + ☐
lilies   tulips

☐ and ☐   7 = ☐ + ☐
lilies   tulips

☐ and ☐   7 = ☐ + ☐
lilies   tulips

☐ and ☐   7 = ☐ + ☐
lilies   tulips

☐ and ☐   7 = ☐ + ☐
lilies   tulips

☐ and ☐   7 = ☐ + ☐
lilies   tulips

Special *Put Together/ Take Apart* Problems

▶ Solve and Discuss

Make a matching drawing or draw comparison bars.
Write an equation. Solve the problem.

Show your work.

1. Ben has 11 library books. If Ben returns 4 books,
he will have as many library books as Dale. How
many library books does Dale have?

library

☐ _____
          label

2. Shelley washes 14 cars. Amir washes 9 cars.
How many **more** cars does Shelley wash
than Amir?

car

☐ _____
          label

3. Gale has 6 peaches in a basket. If Gale gets
5 more peaches, he will have as many peaches
as Carl. How many peaches does Carl have?

basket

☐ _____
          label

4. Rob has 12 stamps. Ann has 5 **fewer** stamps.
How many stamps does Ann have?

stamp

☐ _____
          label

▶ Solve and Discuss (continued)

Make a matching drawing or draw comparison bars.
Write an equation. Solve the problem.

---

5. Helena has 8 toys. If she gets 3 more, she will
have as many toys as Matt. How many toys
does Matt have?

toy

☐ _____
   label

---

6. Martin has 14 plants in his garden. Jacob has
5 fewer plants. How many plants does Jacob have?

garden

☐ _____
   label

---

7. Jana has 12 coins in her coin collection. Ari has
5 fewer coins. How many coins does Ari have?

coin

☐ _____
   label

▶ PATH to FLUENCY Add and Subtract Within 20

Add.

8. $5 + 6 =$ ☐   **9.** $8 + 7 =$ ☐   **10.** $13 + 0 =$ ☐

Subtract.

11. $14 - 6 =$ ☐   **12.** $12 - 3 =$ ☐   **13.** $11 - 9 =$ ☐

Compare Word Problems

© Houghton Mifflin Harcourt Publishing Company

Name _____

▶ Solve and Discuss

Make a drawing. Write an equation.
Solve the problem.

Show your work.

---

1. Haley has 13 books in her bag. Gabrielle
   has 8 books in her bag. How many fewer
   books does Gabrielle have in her bag
   than Haley?

book

[ ] _____
    label

---

2. Hannah has 11 stickers. Nat has 3 stickers.
   How many fewer stickers does Nat have
   than Hannah?

sticker

[ ] _____
    label

---

3. An eraser costs 7 cents. A pencil costs
   9 cents more than an eraser. How many
   cents does a pencil cost?

pencil

[ ] _____
    label

---

4. Linda has 11 cherries. If she eats 4 cherries,
   she will have the same number as Sally.
   How many cherries does Sally have?

cherries

[ ] _____
    label

▶ **Solve and Discuss (continued)**

Make a drawing. Write an equation.
Solve the problem.

Show your work.

5. John has 8 notebooks. He has to get 6 more
notebooks to have as many as Ben.
How many notebooks does Ben have?

notebook

[ ] _____
       label

6. Rasha solves 3 more puzzles than Leena.
Leena solves 9 puzzles. How many
puzzles does Rasha solve?

puzzle

[ ] _____
       label

▶ **What's the Error?**

Latoya has 12 buttons. If she gives away 5 buttons,
she will have as many as Ron. How many buttons
does Ron have?

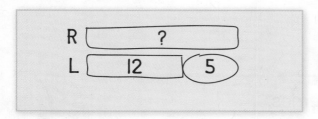

R [?   ]
L [12] (5)

Did I make
a mistake?

7. Draw comparison bars to help Puzzled Penguin.

More *Compare* Word Problems

▶ Solve and Discuss

Make a drawing. Write an equation.
Solve the problem.

Show your work.

---

1. Erica has 13 color pencils. She has 8 at
home and some at school. How many
are at school?

school

☐ _____
label

---

2. Joan has 15 toy guitars. Delia has 7 toy
guitars. How many fewer toy guitars
does Delia have than Joan?

guitar

☐ _____
label

---

3. Ed has 14 puppets. He gives some to
his brother. Now Ed has 5 puppets left.
How many puppets does Ed give to
his brother?

puppet

☐ _____
label

---

4. Yolanda has a box of tennis balls. Alvin
takes 7 of them. Now Yolanda has 5 left.
How many tennis balls does Yolanda
have in the beginning?

box

☐ _____
label

▶ Solve and Discuss (continued)

Make a drawing. Write an equation.
Solve the problem.

Show your work.

---

5. Meena has 6 cherries. Anika gives
   her some more cherries. Meena has
   13 cherries now. How many cherries
   does Anika give Meena?

cherry

☐ _____
      label

---

6. Shane has 16 stamps. Dan has
   7 fewer stamps than Shane. How
   many stamps does Dan have?

stamp

☐ _____
      label

---

7. Lisha wants to put 15 apples in a bowl.
   She wants to use both green apples
   and red apples. How many of each could
   she use? Show three answers.

bowl

☐ green apples and ☐ red apples

☐ green apples and ☐ red apples

☐ green apples and ☐ red apples

Mixed Word Problems

$5 + 7 = \boxed{}$

$6 + 7 = \boxed{}$

$9 + 9 = \boxed{}$

$8 + 7 = \boxed{}$

$9 + 7 = \boxed{}$

$3 + 8 = \boxed{}$

$4 + 8 = \boxed{}$

$5 + 8 = \boxed{}$

$6 + 8 = \boxed{}$

$7 + 8 = \boxed{}$

$8 + 8 = \boxed{}$

$9 + 8 = \boxed{}$

$3 + 9 = \boxed{}$

$4 + 9 = \boxed{}$

$5 + 9 = \boxed{}$

$9 + 9 = \boxed{18}$

9	•	•••••
		•••••

9 + 1 + 8

$6 + 7 = \boxed{13}$

7	•••	•••

7 + 3 + 3

$5 + 7 = \boxed{12}$

7	•••	••

7 + 3 + 2

$3 + 8 = \boxed{11}$

8	••	•

8 + 2 + 1

$9 + 7 = \boxed{16}$

9	•	•••••

9 + 1 + 6

$8 + 7 = \boxed{15}$

8	••	•••••

8 + 2 + 5

$6 + 8 = \boxed{14}$

8	••	••••

8 + 2 + 4

$5 + 8 = \boxed{13}$

8	••	•••

8 + 2 + 3

$4 + 8 = \boxed{12}$

8	••	••

8 + 2 + 2

$9 + 8 = \boxed{17}$

9	•	•••••
		••

9 + 1 + 7

$8 + 8 = \boxed{16}$

8	••	•••••
		•

8 + 2 + 6

$7 + 8 = \boxed{15}$

8	••	•••••

8 + 2 + 5

$5 + 9 = \boxed{14}$

9	•	••••

9 + 1 + 4

$4 + 9 = \boxed{13}$

9	•	•••

9 + 1 + 3

$3 + 9 = \boxed{12}$

9	•	••

9 + 1 + 2

Green Make-a-Ten Cards

6 + 9 = ☐

7 + 9 = ☐

7 + 4 = ☐

8 + 4 = ☐

9 + 4 = ☐

6 + 5 = ☐

7 + 5 = ☐

8 + 5 = ☐

9 + 5 = ☐

5 + 6 = ☐

8 + 9 = ☐

7 + 6 = ☐

8 + 6 = ☐

9 + 6 = ☐

4 + 7 = ☐

$7 + 4 = \boxed{11}$

| 7 | ••• • |

7 + 3 + 1

$7 + 9 = \boxed{16}$

| 9 | • ••••• |

9 + 1 + 6

$6 + 9 = \boxed{15}$

| 9 | • ••••• |

9 + 1 + 5

$6 + 5 = \boxed{11}$

| 6 | •••• • |

6 + 4 + 1

$9 + 4 = \boxed{13}$

| 9 | • ••• |

9 + 1 + 3

$8 + 4 = \boxed{12}$

| 8 | •• •• |

8 + 2 + 2

$9 + 5 = \boxed{14}$

| 9 | • •••• |

9 + 1 + 4

$8 + 5 = \boxed{13}$

| 8 | •• ••• |

8 + 2 + 3

$7 + 5 = \boxed{12}$

| 7 | ••• •• |

7 + 3 + 2

$7 + 6 = \boxed{13}$

| 7 | ••• ••• |

7 + 3 + 3

$8 + 9 = \boxed{17}$

| 9 | • ••••• • |

9 + 1 + 7

$5 + 6 = \boxed{11}$

| 6 | •••• • |

6 + 4 + 1

$4 + 7 = \boxed{11}$

| 7 | ••• • |

7 + 3 + 1

$9 + 6 = \boxed{15}$

| 9 | • ••••• |

9 + 1 + 5

$8 + 6 = \boxed{14}$

| 8 | •• •••• |

8 + 2 + 4

Green Make-a-Ten Cards

► Complete and Solve Word Problems

Add information so you can solve the problems.
Then solve the problem.

Show your work.

---

1. Shannon makes a pitcher of lemonade. She uses
   8 lemons. How many lemons does she have left?

pitcher

_____

☐ _____
　　label

---

2. Sam walks his dog in the morning and again in
   the afternoon. Altogether Sam and the dog walk
   15 blocks. How far do they walk in the morning?

dog

_____

☐ _____
　　label

---

3. Kari makes a bracelet with blue and purple beads.
   6 beads are blue. How many beads are purple?

beads

_____

☐ _____
　　label

VOCABULARY
extra information

▶ Solve Problems with Extra Information

Cross out the **extra information**. Solve.

Show your work.

---

4. The dentist has 8 red toothbrushes and 6 green ones. Then she buys 9 more red ones. How many red toothbrushes does she have now?

◻ _____
    label

toothbrush

---

5. Rosa has 5 gold coins and 6 silver coins in her collection. Her brother gives her 7 more gold coins. How many gold coins does Rosa have in all?

◻ _____
    label

coin

---

6. Pam has 7 long ribbons and 9 short ribbons. She gives away 5 short ones. How many short ribbons does Pam have now?

◻ _____
    label

ribbon

---

7. Franny has 8 kittens and 2 dogs. 4 kittens are asleep. How many kittens are awake?

◻ _____
    label

dog

Name _____

► **Find Information in a Story**

> ### The Zoo
> Today my class went to the zoo. I saw 4 elephants and 5 tigers. The giraffes were tall. There were 8 monkeys playing. I counted 13 penguins. I had fun at the zoo.
>
> By Robbie

Use the story to solve the problems.   **Show your work.**

8. How many more monkeys than tigers did Robbie see?

☐ _____
　　label

monkey

9. How many more penguins than elephants did Robbie see?

☐ _____
　　label

elephant

10. How many fewer tigers than penguins did Robbie see?

☐ _____
　　label

penguin

VOCABULARY
hidden information

▶ Practice Solving Word Problems

Cross out extra information or write missing or
hidden information. Solve the problem.

Show your work.

---

11. Chris washes some cars at the car wash. His friend
Kelly washes some cars at the car wash. They
wash a total of 16 cars. How many cars did
Kelly wash?

car wash

_____

☐ _____

label

---

12. Shanna puts 13 markers and 6 crayons in her
book bag. When she gets to school, she gives
4 of the markers to her friend. How many markers
does Shanna have left?

marker

_____

☐ _____

label

---

13. There are 9 children and a set of triplets in the
library. How many children are in the library?

library

_____

☐ _____

label

Problems with Not Enough, Extra, or Hidden Information

► Solve and Discuss

Draw comparison bars. Write an equation.
Solve the problem.

Show your work.

---

1. Darnell has 6 pens. That is 5 fewer pens
than Natasha. How many pens does
Natasha have?

pen

☐ _____
     label

---

2. There are 8 tigers at the Smithfield Zoo.
The zoo has 9 more lions than tigers.
How many lions does the zoo have?

tiger

☐ _____
     label

---

3. Sherean saves $7 more in October than
in September. She saves $15 in October.
How many dollars does she save
in September?

dollar

☐ _____
     label

---

4. Nayoki makes 8 fewer airplane models
than Maria. If Nayoki makes 9 airplane
models, how many does Maria make?

airplane
model

☐ _____
     label

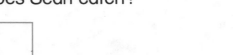

▶ Solve and Discuss (continued)

Draw comparison bars. Write an equation.
Solve the problem.

Show your work.

5. Chris catches 15 fish. Sean catches
   9 fewer fish than Chris. How many fish
   does Sean catch?

fish

   □ _____
          label

6. There are 9 more apples in the basket
   than bananas. There are 17 apples in
   the basket. How many bananas are in the
   basket?

basket

   □ _____
          label

7. Maya has 8 fewer pennies than nickels.
   How many nickels does she have if she
   has 7 pennies?

nickel

   □ _____
          label

8. There are 5 more horses in the barn
   than the field. There are 12 horses in the
   barn. How many horses are in the field?

barn

   □ _____
          label

More Complex *Compare* Problems

▶ Model Two-Step Word Problems

Solve the two-step word problem.   **Show your work.**

1. Lindsay brings in 5 cans for the school food drive.
   Olivia brings in 4 more cans than Lindsay. Matt
   brings in 6 more cans than Olivia. How many cans
   does Matt bring?

A. How many cans does Olivia bring?

☐ _____
      label

B. How many cans does Matt bring?

☐ _____
      label

▶ Model Two-Step Word Problems (continued)

Solve the two-step word problem.

Show your work.

2. There are 14 computers in the school library. 5 girls and 3 boys are each using a computer right now. How many more children can use a computer?

A. How many children are using computers right now?

☐ _____
label

B. How many more children can use a computer?

☐ _____
label

Two-Step Word Problems

► Solve Two-Step Word Problems

Think about the first-step question.
Then solve the problem.

Show your work.

3. Mari has 17 tomatoes. She uses 9 tomatoes to make a sauce. Then she makes a salad with 4 tomatoes. How many tomatoes does she have left?

tomato

☐ _____
      label

4. There are 16 robins in a tree. 9 robins fly away. Then 4 blue jays fly into the tree. How many birds are in the tree now?

robin

☐ _____
      label

5. Julie has 6 red pencils. She has 2 more blue pencils than red pencils. How many pencils does she have in all?

pencil

☐ _____
      label

▶ Solve Two-Step Word Problems (continued)

Think about the first-step question.
Then solve the problem.

Show your work.

6. Lana had 9 sheep and some horses on her farm. Altogether there were 17 animals. Her grandmother gives her 3 more horses. How many horses does she have on the farm now?

sheep

◻ _____
        label

7. Rafa has 13 marbles. He has 6 red marbles and the rest are green. Mia gives him some more green marbles. Now Rafa has 12 green marbles. How many green marbles does Mia give Rafa?

marbles

◻ _____
        label

▶ (PATH to FLUENCY) Add and Subtract Within 20

Add.

8. $4 + 6 =$ ◻   9. $5 + 7 =$ ◻   10. $9 + 6 =$ ◻

Subtract.

11. $18 - 9 =$ ◻   12. $12 - 8 =$ ◻   13. $11 - 3 =$ ◻

▶ Solve and Discuss

Make a drawing. Write an equation.
Solve the problem.

Show your work.

1. Mina buys some new shirts. She returns 4 shirts to the store. Now she has 8 new shirts. How many shirts does Mina buy at first?

store

_____ label

2. Marie buys 8 peaches and a dozen apples. That is 6 fewer peaches than Rubin buys. How many peaches does Rubin buy?

peach

_____ label

3. There are 17 children in the class play. 9 are boys and the rest are girls. Then 3 more girls join the play. How many girls are in the play?

children

_____ label

4. Ed buys 9 books at one store and 3 books at another. He buys 8 more books than Brenda. How many books does Brenda buy?

book

_____ label

► **Solve and Discuss (continued)**

Make a drawing. Write an equation.
Solve the problem.

Show your work.

---

5. There are some cows in a field. 4 horses join them.
   Now there are 12 animals in the field. How many
   cows are in the field?

horse

[ ] _____
         label

---

6. Rob sells 6 skateboards on Friday, 3 skateboards on
   Saturday, and 2 skateboards on Sunday. How many
   skateboards does he sell altogether?

skateboard

[ ] _____
         label

► **What's the Error?**

Felix has 7 white potatoes, 8 purple potatoes,
and 5 green apples. He uses all the potatoes to
make a soup. How many potatoes does Felix use?

$$7 + 8 + 5 = 20 \text{ potatoes}$$
w   p   g

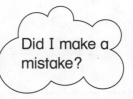
Did I make a mistake?

7. Help Puzzled Penguin.

$$15 - 6 = \boxed{}$$

$$16 - 7 = \boxed{}$$

$$11 - 7 = \boxed{}$$

$$12 - 8 = \boxed{}$$

$$13 - 9 = \boxed{}$$

$$11 - 6 = \boxed{}$$

$$12 - 7 = \boxed{}$$

$$13 - 8 = \boxed{}$$

$$14 - 9 = \boxed{}$$

$$11 - 5 = \boxed{}$$

$$17 - 8 = \boxed{}$$

$$13 - 7 = \boxed{}$$

$$14 - 8 = \boxed{}$$

$$15 - 9 = \boxed{}$$

$$11 - 4 = \boxed{}$$

$$11 - 7 = 4$$
$$3$$
$$1$$

$$16 - 7 = 9$$
$$3$$
$$6$$

$$15 - 6 = 9$$
$$4$$
$$5$$

$$11 - 6 = 5$$
$$4$$
$$1$$

$$13 - 9 = 4$$
$$1$$
$$3$$

$$12 - 8 = 4$$
$$2$$
$$2$$

$$14 - 9 = 5$$
$$1$$
$$4$$

$$13 - 8 = 5$$
$$2$$
$$3$$

$$12 - 7 = 5$$
$$3$$
$$2$$

$$13 - 7 = 6$$
$$3$$
$$3$$

$$17 - 8 = 9$$
$$2$$
$$7$$

$$11 - 5 = 6$$
$$5$$
$$1$$

$$11 - 4 = 7$$
$$6$$
$$1$$

$$15 - 9 = 6$$
$$1$$
$$5$$

$$14 - 8 = 6$$
$$2$$
$$4$$

Blue Make-a-Ten Cards

12 − 5 = ☐　　13 − 6 = ☐　　18 − 9 = ☐

15 − 8 = ☐　　16 − 9 = ☐　　11 − 3 = ☐

12 − 4 = ☐　　13 − 5 = ☐　　14 − 6 = ☐

15 − 7 = ☐　　16 − 8 = ☐　　17 − 9 = ☐

12 − 3 = ☐　　13 − 4 = ☐　　14 − 5 = ☐

$18 - 9 = \boxed{9}$
1
8

$13 - 6 = \boxed{7}$
4
3

$12 - 5 = \boxed{7}$
5
2

$11 - 3 = \boxed{8}$
7
1

$16 - 9 = \boxed{7}$
1
6

$15 - 8 = \boxed{7}$
2
5

$14 - 6 = \boxed{8}$
4
4

$13 - 5 = \boxed{8}$
5
3

$12 - 4 = \boxed{8}$
6
2

$17 - 9 = \boxed{8}$
1
7

$16 - 8 = \boxed{8}$
2
6

$15 - 7 = \boxed{8}$
3
5

$14 - 5 = \boxed{9}$
5
4

$13 - 4 = \boxed{9}$
6
3

$12 - 3 = \boxed{9}$
7
2

Blue Make-a-Ten Cards

Name _____

► **Math and Healthy Food**

Beren and her friends are making funny face pizzas.

1. Darryl uses 2 green olives for eyes and 9 black olives to make a big smile. How many olives does he use?

[ ] _____
   label

2. Sarah uses 6 fewer mushroom slices than Darryl. Sarah uses 8 slices. How many slices does Darryl use?

[ ] _____
   label

3. When they start making the pizzas, there are a dozen small tomatoes. Darryl uses 2 tomatoes. Beren and Dawn each use 1 tomato. No one else uses any. How many tomatoes are left?

[ ] _____
   label

▶ Problems with Extra Information

Solve. Cross out the information you do not need.   Show your work.

4. Beren makes a fruit salad. She uses 2 strawberries,
   8 blueberries, 7 raspberries, and 3 apples.
   How many berries does she use?

   ☐ _____
   　　　　label

5. Darryl makes a snack mix. He uses 2 cups of cereal,
   4 cups of raisins, 3 cups of dried cherries, and
   2 cups of walnuts. How many more cups of dried fruit
   does he use than cups of nuts?

   ☐ _____
   　　　　label

▶ Write and Solve a Problem

"Ants on a Log" is a snack made with celery, peanut butter,
and raisins.

Beren's Snack

Darryl's Snack

Sarah's Snack

6. Use the pictures. On a separate sheet of paper, write
   a problem.

   Exchange with a classmate. Solve each other's problem.

Solve.

1. $8 + 0 = \boxed{}$

2. $\boxed{} = 7 + 8$

3. $\boxed{} = 9 + 5$

4. $7 + 5 = \boxed{}$

5. $6 + \boxed{} = 13$

6. $\boxed{} + 9 = 11$

7. $17 - 8 = \boxed{}$

8. $16 - 8 = \boxed{}$

9. $4 + 7 + 6 = \boxed{}$

10. $9 + 4 = \boxed{}$

11. $7 + 4 + 3 + 6 = \boxed{}$

Add.

12. $\begin{array}{r} 9 \\ + 3 \\ \hline \end{array}$

Subtract.

13. $\begin{array}{r} 11 \\ - 6 \\ \hline \end{array}$

Solve.   **Show your work.**

14. Jenna has 11 balloons. She gives some balloons to her friend. Now she has only 7 balloons. How many balloons does she give to her friend?

☐ _____
        label

15. There are 12 sheep at a farm. 5 sheep are in the pen. The rest are in the field. How many sheep are in the field?

☐ _____
        label

16. Jaya has 16 dolls. Reba has 7 dolls. How many fewer dolls does Reba have?

☐ _____
        label

17. Jim has 4 roses, 8 tulips, and 8 daisies. He puts all the roses and the tulips in a vase. How many flowers does he put in the vase?

☐ _____
        label

Solve.   Show your work.

18. Makala buys 9 plums. That is 7 fewer plums than
Trin buys. How many plums does Trin buy?

☐ _____
        label

19. Joey has a bag of peanuts. He gives 8 peanuts
to Sandy. Now he has 7 peanuts left. How many
peanuts are in the bag in the beginning?

☐ _____
        label

20. There are 6 elephants, 4 lions, and 4 horses at
an animal park. How many animals are at the
animal park?

☐ _____
        label

21. Clint picks 13 apples. Tim picks 5 fewer apples than
Clint picks. How many apples does Tim pick?

☐ _____
        label

Solve.   **Show your work.**

22. There are some puzzle pieces on the table. Kay puts 9 more on the table. Now there are 17 pieces on the table. How many puzzle pieces were on the table at first?

    ☐ _____
          label

23. Darnell sells 14 baseball caps. He sells 5 more than Amelia. How many baseball caps does Amelia sell?

    ☐ _____
          label

24. There are 5 puppies, 3 rabbits, and some kittens at an animal shelter. There are a total of 15 animals at the shelter. How many kittens are at the animal shelter?

    ☐ _____
          label

25. **Extended Response** Choose an even number. Write a doubles addition equation for your number. Explain how you know the number is even.

    _____

    _____

    _____

Dear Family:

Your child is learning about place value and will use this knowledge to add 2- and 3-digit numbers.

As we begin this unit, your child will represent numbers using drawings like this one:

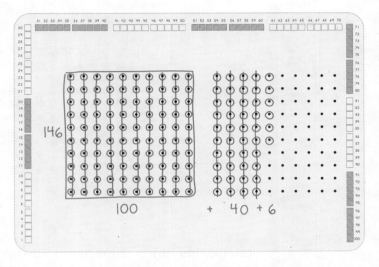

Then, children will begin to represent numbers using Quick Hundreds and Quick Tens.

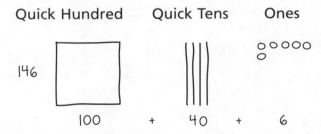

Quick Hundred   Quick Tens   Ones

146   100   +   40   +   6

Name a 2- or 3-digit number and ask your child to make a drawing to represent that number.

Later in this unit, children will work on adding 2-digit numbers using the drawings to help them.

Thank you. Please call or write if you have any questions.

Sincerely,
Your child's teacher

COMMON CORE   Unit 2 includes the Common Core Standards for Mathematical Content for Operations and Algebraic Thinking, 2.OA.1, 2.OA.2; Number and Operations in Base Ten, 2.NBT.1, 2.NBT.1a, 2.NBT.1b, 2.NBT.2, 2.NBT.3, 2.NBT.4, 2.NBT.5, 2.NBT.6, 2.NBT.7, 2.NBT.8, 2.NBT.9; Measurement and Data, 2.MD.8; and all Mathematical Practices.

Estimada familia:

Su niño está aprendiendo acerca del valor posicional y usará esos conocimientos para sumar números de 2 y 3 dígitos.

Cuando comencemos con esta unidad, su niño representará números usando dibujos como este:

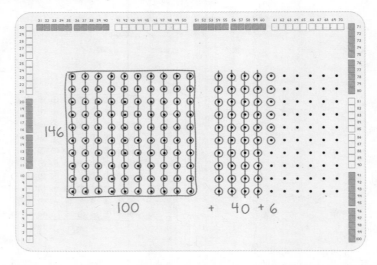

Luego, los niños comenzarán a representar números usando "Centenas rápidas" y "Decenas rápidas".

Centena rápida   Decenas rápidas   Unidades

146   100   +   40   +   6

Diga un número de 2 ó 3 dígitos y pida a su niño que haga un dibujo para representar ese número.

Más adelante, los niños trabajarán sumando números de 2 dígitos y usarán los dibujos como ayuda.

Gracias. Si tiene alguna pregunta, por favor comuníquese conmigo.

Atentamente,
El maestro de su niño

COMMON CORE

La Unidad 2 incluye los Common Core Standards for Mathematical Content for Operations and Algebraic Thinking, 2.OA.1, 2.OA.2; Number and Operations in Base Ten, 2.NBT.1, 2.NBT.1a, 2.NBT.1b, 2.NBT.2, 2.NBT.3, 2.NBT.4, 2.NBT.5, 2.NBT.6, 2.NBT.7, 2.NBT.8, 2.NBT.9; Measurement and Data, 2.MD.8; and all Mathematical Practices.

▶ Write the Numbers 101 to 200

1. Write the numbers going down to see the tens.

101	111								
102		122			152				
103						163			193
				144					
								185	
	116				156				
		128							
								189	
110	120			150		170			200

▶ Word Problem Practice: Addition and Subtraction Within 20

Solve.   **Show your work.**

2. Sara has some marbles. Shane gives her 8 more marbles. Now Sara has 17 marbles. How many marbles did Sara have at first?

   ☐ _____
        label

   marbles

3. There are 14 children on the soccer field. There are 8 boys and the rest are girls. Then 2 girls leave the soccer field. How many girls are on the soccer field now?

   ☐ _____
        label

   soccer field

4. Tom has 6 fewer pencils than Ari. Tom has 7 pencils. How many pencils does Ari have?

   ☐ _____
        label

   pencil

5. In the lunchroom, 16 children have apples. Nine of these children have red apples and the rest have green apples. Then 5 more children come with green apples. How many children have green apples now?

   ☐ _____
        label

   apple

Ones, Tens, and Hundreds

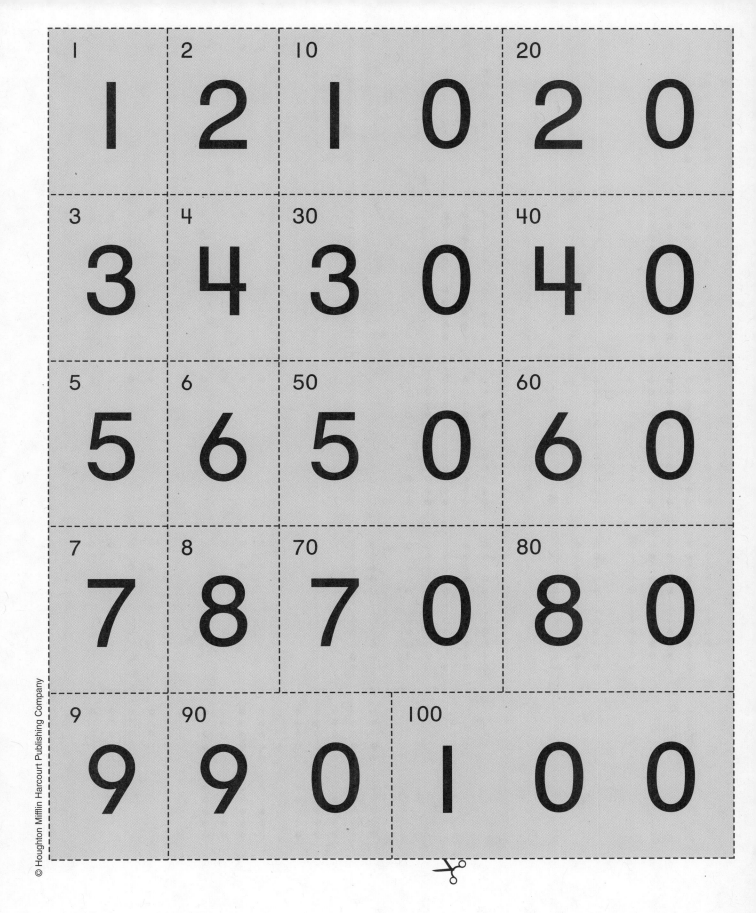

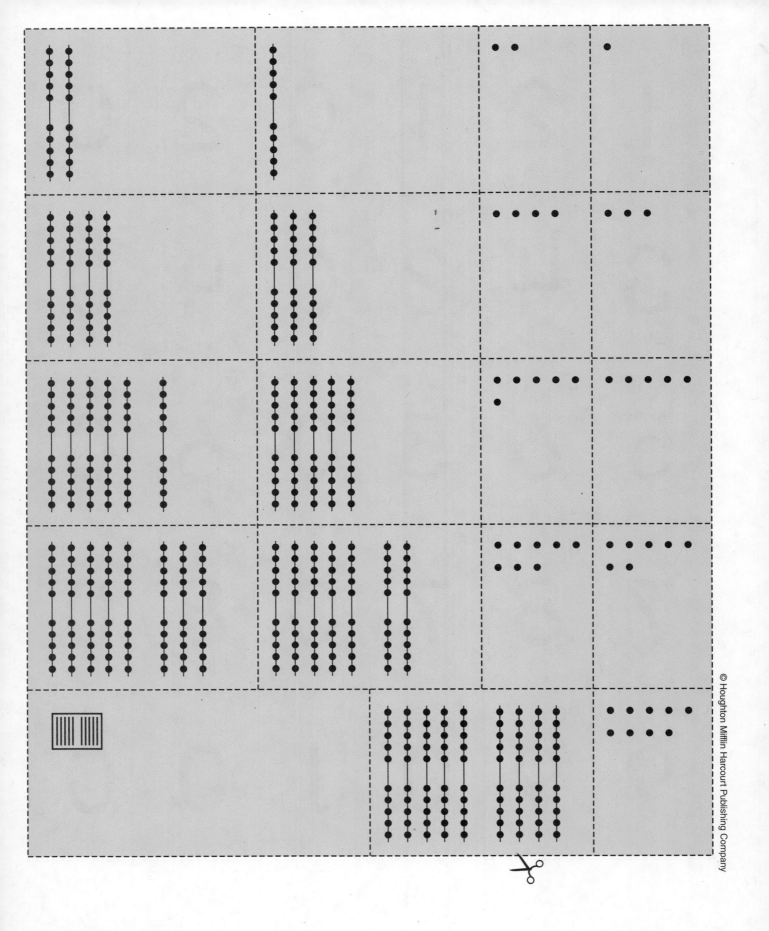

Secret Code Cards (1–100)

▶ Add Tens or Ones

Add.

1. 10 + 20 = _30_   70 + 20 = _90_   60 + 30 = _90_

  1 + 2 = _3_   7 + 2 = _9_   6 + 3 = _9_

2. 20 + 70 = _90_   30 + 50 = _80_   40 + 50 = _90_

  2 + 7 = _9_   3 + 5 = _8_   4 + 5 = _9_

3. 30 + 60 = _90_   20 + 80 = _100_   50 + 40 = _90_

  3 + 6 = _9_   2 + 8 = _10_   5 + 4 = _9_

4. 50 + 50 = _100_   80 + 20 = _100_   40 + 60 = _100_

  5 + 5 = _10_   8 + 2 = _10_   4 + 6 = _10_

5. 90 + 10 = _100_   90 + 20 = _111_   40 + 30 = _70_

  9 + 1 = _10_   9 + 2 = _11_   4 + 3 = _1_

6. 50 + 20 = _70_   20 + 30 = _50_   60 + 70 = _113_

  5 + 2 = _1_   2 + 3 = _5_   6 + 7 = _13_

► Word Problem Practice: Addition and Subtraction Within 20

Solve.

Show your work.

7. There are 18 children in the library. 9 children leave the library. Then 3 more children come. How many children are in the library now?

library

  _____
label

8. Some crayons are on the table. Mrs. Spain takes 5 of the crayons. Now there are 8 crayons on the table. How many crayons were on the table before?

crayon

  _____
label

9. The jewelry store has 8 red bracelets and some blue bracelets. There are 15 bracelets in all. Then 3 blue bracelets are sold. How many blue bracelets are still in the store?

bracelet

  _____
label

10. Mr. Rivera bakes 7 banana muffins and 9 orange muffins. He gives some muffins to his friends. Now he has 8 muffins. How many muffins does he give to his friends?

muffin

  _____
label

▶ Hundreds, Tens, and Ones

Draw the number using hundred boxes, ten sticks, and
circles. Then write the **expanded form**.

1. ☐ ○○○○○ ○	**2.**	**3.**
106	122	139
100 + 0 + 6	100 + 2 + 2	100 + 3 + 99

What number is shown?

H = Hundreds, T = Tens, O = Ones

4. ☐ ‖‖‖‖ ○○○○○ ○○

___1___ H ___4___ T ___7___ O

147 = 100 + 40 + 7

5. ☐ ‖‖‖‖‖‖‖ ○

___1___ H ___7___ T ___1___ O

___ = ___ + ___ + ___

6. ☐ ‖‖‖‖‖‖

___1___ H ___6___ T ___0___ O

100 = 0 + 6 + 100

7. ☐ ‖‖‖‖‖‖‖‖‖ ○○○○○ ○○○○

___1___ H ___9___ T ___9___ O

199 = 9 + 9 + 100

▶ Read and Write Number Names

1 one	11 eleven	10 ten	100 one hundred
2 two	12 twelve	20 twenty	
3 three	13 thirteen	30 thirty	
4 four	14 fourteen	40 forty	
5 five	15 fifteen	50 fifty	
6 six	16 sixteen	60 sixty	
7 seven	17 seventeen	70 seventy	
8 eight	18 eighteen	80 eighty	
9 nine	19 nineteen	90 ninety	

Write the number.

8. thirty-five _____

9. seventy-two _____

10. fifty-four _____

11. eighty-nine _____

12. sixty-three _____

13. ninety-one _____

Write the **number name**.

14. 47 _____

15. 62 _____

16. 85 _____

17. 94 _____

18. 28 _____

19. 86 _____

Represent Write the number name, then draw Quick Tens and ones in the box.

20. 60 _____

21. 72 _____

Represent Numbers in Different Ways

▶ Word Problems with Groups of Ten

Solve. Make a proof drawing.   **Show your work.**

---

1. Remah has 34 stickers. Only 10 stickers fit on a
page in her scrapbook. How many pages can she fill
with stickers? How many stickers will be left over?

[ ] pages   [ ] stickers left over

---

2. David has 42 beads. He wants to make some
necklaces that use 10 beads each. How many
necklaces can he make? How many beads will
be left over?

[ ] necklaces   [ ] beads left over

---

3. The team wants to buy T-shirts that cost 10 dollars
each. They have 57 dollars. How many T-shirts can
they buy? How many dollars will be left over?

[ ] T-shirts   [ ] dollars left over

---

4. The store has 163 apples. Each basket can hold
10 apples. How many baskets can they fill with
apples? How many apples will be left over?

[ ] baskets   [ ] apples left over

► **Add 1, 10, or 100**

Add.

5. $38 + 1 =$ _____

6. $9 + 10 =$ _____

7. $24 + 100 =$ _____

8. $150 + 1 =$ _____

9. $7 + 100 =$ _____

10. $92 + 10 =$ _____

11. $59 + 1 =$ _____

12. $166 + 10 =$ _____

13. $10 + 10 =$ _____

14. $143 + 1 =$ _____

15. $98 + 100 =$ _____

16. $46 + 10 =$ _____

17. $11 + 100 =$ _____

18. $195 + 1 =$ _____

19. $104 + 10 =$ _____

20. $30 + 100 =$ _____

VOCABULARY
is less than ($<$)
is greater than ($>$)
is equal to ($=$)

▶ Use Drawings to Compare Numbers

Use these symbols to compare numbers.

$<$ **is less than** $>$ **is greater than** $=$ **is equal to**

Make a drawing for each number. Write $<$, $>$, or $=$.

1.   56 ◯ 81

2.   123 ◯ 109

3.   101 ◯ 101

4.   98 150

5.   67 ◯ 76

6.   120 102

▶ Compare Numbers

Write <, >, or =.

7. 135 (<) 137

8. 83 (=) 83

9. 119 (>) 87

10. 127 (<) 172

11. 62 (>) 57

12. 51 (>) 15

13. 111 (=) 111

14. 37 (<) 74

15. 192 (>) 191

16. 100 (>) 10

▶ What's the Error?

149 (>) 176

I know that 9 is greater than 6. Did I make a mistake?

17. Draw a proof drawing to help Puzzled Penguin.
   Write <, >, or =.

149 (<) 176

Family Letter

Dear Family:

Your child is now learning how to add 2-digit numbers. The "big mystery" in adding is making a new ten or a new hundred. Children can write this new group in several ways.

Show All Totals	New Groups Below
$$\begin{array}{r} 45 \\ + 28 \\ \hline \end{array}$$ Add tens. → 60 Add ones. → 13 $$\begin{array}{r}\hline 73 \end{array}$$ Find total tens. Find total ones.	$$\begin{array}{r} 45 \\ + 28 \\ \hline 73 \end{array}$$ New ten

(Show All Totals) New ten

(New Groups Below) Find total ones. (13) Write 3 and put the new ten in the tens column ready to add.

Add the tens. (4 + 2 = 6, 6 + 1 = 7)

Children usually find it easier to write the new ten below because then they add the new ten last. They add 4 + 2 = 6 and then 6 + 1 = 7.

Traditionally, most children have learned to write the new ten above. With this method, you add 1 + 4 = 5 and then 5 + 2 = 7. This is more difficult for many children, but some children may still choose this method, particularly if they have been taught to do so previously.

Thank you for helping your child learn mathematics.

Sincerely,
Your child's teacher

New Groups Above

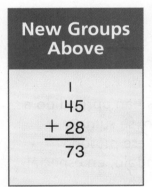

$$\begin{array}{r} 1 \\ 45 \\ + 28 \\ \hline 73 \end{array}$$

COMMON CORE

Unit 2 includes the Common Core Standards for Mathematical Content for Operations and Algebraic Thinking, 2.OA.1, 2.OA.2; Number and Operations in Base Ten, 2.NBT.1, 2.NBT.1a, 2.NBT.1b, 2.NBT.2, 2.NBT.3, 2.NBT.4, 2.NBT.5, 2.NBT.6, 2.NBT.7, 2.NBT.8, 2.NBT.9; Measurement and Data, 2.MD.8; and all Mathematical Practices.

Carta a la familia

Estimada familia:

Su niño está aprendiendo a sumar números de 2 dígitos. El "gran misterio" en la suma de números de 2 dígitos consiste en formar una nueva decena o una nueva centena. Los niños pueden anotar este nuevo grupo de varias maneras.

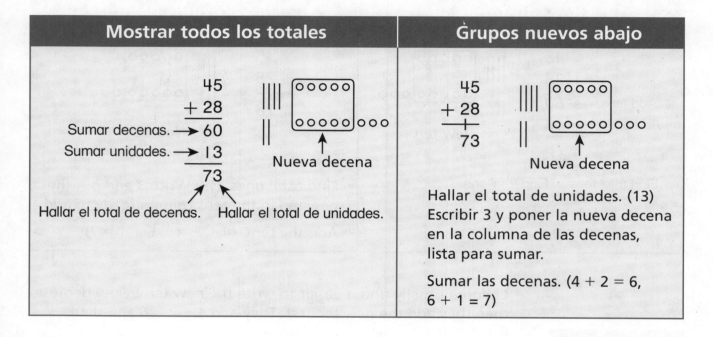

Mostrar todos los totales	Grupos nuevos abajo
$$\begin{array}{r} 45 \\ +\ 28 \\ \hline \end{array}$$ Sumar decenas. → 60 Sumar unidades. → 13 $$\begin{array}{r} \hline 73 \end{array}$$ Hallar el total de decenas. Hallar el total de unidades. **Nueva decena**	$$\begin{array}{r} 45 \\ +\ 28 \\ \hline 73 \end{array}$$ **Nueva decena** Hallar el total de unidades. (13) Escribir 3 y poner la nueva decena en la columna de las decenas, lista para sumar. Sumar las decenas. (4 + 2 = 6, 6 + 1 = 7)

Por lo general a los niños les resulta más fácil escribir la nueva decena abajo, porque entonces suman la nueva decena al final. Suman 4 + 2 = 6 y luego 6 + 1 = 7.

Tradicionalmente, la mayoría de los estudiantes han aprendido a escribir la nueva decena arriba. Con ese método, se suma 1 + 4 = 5 y luego 5 + 2 = 7. Para muchos niños ese método resulta más difícil pero algunos siguen escogiéndolo, en especial si ya lo han aprendido.

Gracias por ayudar a su niño a aprender matemáticas.

Atentamente,
El maestro de su niño

Grupos nuevos arriba

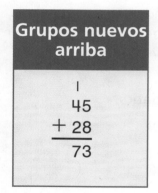

$$\begin{array}{r} 1 \\ 45 \\ +\ 28 \\ \hline 73 \end{array}$$

© Houghton Mifflin Harcourt Publishing Company

COMMON CORE

La Unidad 2 incluye los Common Core Standards for Mathematical Content for Operations and Algebraic Thinking, 2.OA.1, 2.OA.2; Number and Operations in Base Ten, 2.NBT.1, 2.NBT.1a, 2.NBT.1b, 2.NBT.2, 2.NBT.3, 2.NBT.4, 2.NBT.5, 2.NBT.6, 2.NBT.7, 2.NBT.8, 2.NBT.9; Measurement and Data, 2.MD.8; and all Mathematical Practices.

▶The New Ten

Solve each word problem.

1. Mr. Green puts 56 red peppers in the vegetable bin. Mrs. Green puts 28 yellow peppers in the bin. How many peppers do they put in the bin altogether?

☐ _____
　　　　　label

2. Mrs. Green stacks 43 tomatoes. Mr. Green adds 39 more. How many tomatoes do they stack in all?

☐ _____
　　　　　label

▶The New Hundred

3. Mr. Green counts 65 cans. Mrs. Green counts 82 cans. How many cans do they count in all?

☐ _____
　　　　　label

4. Mrs. Green counts 57 bags of beans. Mr. Green counts 71 bags of beans. How many bags of beans do they count in all?

☐ _____
　　　　　label

► Make a Ten or Hundred

Solve each word problem.

Show your work.

5. Mrs. Green stacks 37 boxes of mushrooms.
   Mr. Green stacks 29 boxes of mushrooms.
   How many boxes do they stack altogether?

   ☐ _____
   label

6. Mr. Green sells 65 bananas.
   Mrs. Green sells 54 bananas.
   How many bananas do they sell in all?

   ☐ _____
   label

► PATH to FLUENCY Add and Subtract Within 20

Add.

7. $6 + 8 =$ _____

8. $9 + 7 =$ _____

9. $6 + 10 =$ _____

10. $\begin{array}{r} 9 \\ + 4 \\ \hline \end{array}$

11. $\begin{array}{r} 10 \\ + 1 \\ \hline \end{array}$

12. $\begin{array}{r} 7 \\ + 6 \\ \hline \end{array}$

Subtract.

13. $15 - 7 =$ _____

14. $20 - 10 =$ _____

15. $18 - 9 =$ _____

16. $\begin{array}{r} 11 \\ - 6 \\ \hline \end{array}$

17. $\begin{array}{r} 15 \\ - 8 \\ \hline \end{array}$

18. $\begin{array}{r} 16 \\ - 7 \\ \hline \end{array}$

Explore 2-Digit Addition

▶ Show All Totals Method

Solve. Make a proof drawing.

Show your work.

1. Mr. Green orders 25 jars of grape jelly and 48 jars of strawberry jelly. How many jars of jelly does he order?

   ☐☐☐ _____
   label

2. Mrs. Green orders 65 pounds of bananas. That is not enough, so she orders 29 more pounds. How many pounds does she order altogether?

   ☐☐☐ _____
   label

3. Mrs. Green orders 78 pounds of white rice and 57 pounds of brown rice. How many pounds of rice does she order?

   ☐☐☐ _____
   label

4. Mr. Green orders 49 jars of plain peanut butter and 86 jars of chunky peanut butter. How many jars of peanut butter does he order in all?

   ☐☐☐ _____
   label

► Word Problem Practice: Two-Step Problems

Solve.   **Show your work.**

5. There were 17 plums on the table. Nine plums were sold. Mr. Green puts some more plums on the table. Now there are 13 plums. How many plums did Mr. Green put on the table?

plum

☐ _____
      label

6. Some carrots are in a basket. Fran adds 5 more carrots to the basket. James places 4 more carrots there. Now there are 13 carrots. How many carrots were in the basket in the beginning?

carrots

☐ _____
      label

7. Jane buys 8 bananas. Damon buys 4 fewer bananas than Jane. How many bananas do they buy in all?

bananas

☐ _____
      label

8. There were 7 bags of green grapes and some bags of red grapes. There were 15 bags of grapes in all. Then 3 bags of red grapes were sold. How many bags of red grapes are left?

grapes

☐ _____
      label

Addition—Show All Totals Method

► Practice and Share

Add. Use any method.

$$
\begin{array}{r}
86 \\
+\ 57 \\
\hline
130 \\
+\ 13 \\
\hline
143
\end{array}
\quad \text{or} \quad
\begin{array}{r}
86 \\
+\ 57 \\
\hline
143
\end{array}
$$

$$130 + 13 = 143$$

1.
$$
\begin{array}{r}
39 \\
+97 \\
\hline
136
\end{array}
\qquad
\begin{array}{r}
83 \\
+39 \\
\hline
122
\end{array}
$$

2.
$$
\begin{array}{r}
58 \\
+87 \\
\hline
145
\end{array}
\qquad
\begin{array}{r}
72 \\
+37 \\
\hline
109
\end{array}
$$

3.
$$
\begin{array}{r}
49 \\
+85 \\
\hline
134
\end{array}
\qquad
\begin{array}{r}
94 \\
+52 \\
\hline
146
\end{array}
$$

▶ Predict New Ten or New Hundred

Add. Use any method.

4.   61
    +37

     53
    +98

5.   42
    +80

     66
    +27

▶ What's the Error?

    38
  + 46
  ────
    74

I know that 3 tens plus 4 tens equals 7 tens. Did I make a mistake?

6. Show Puzzled Penguin how you would add the numbers.
   Draw a proof diagram to check your work.

      38
    + 46

Practice Addition with Sums Over 100

► **What's the Error?**

$$\begin{array}{r} 32 \\ + 25 \\ \hline 67 \end{array}$$

Did I make a mistake?

1. Add. Make a proof drawing.

$$\begin{array}{r} 32 \\ + 25 \\ \hline \end{array}$$

$$\begin{array}{r} 48 \\ + 43 \\ \hline 8\ 11 \end{array}$$

Is this correct?

2. Add. Make a proof drawing.

$$\begin{array}{r} 48 \\ + 43 \\ \hline \end{array}$$

▶ What's the Error? (continued)

$$\overset{1}{1}7$$
$$+\ 66$$
$$\overline{74}$$

Is this one correct?

3. Add. Make a proof drawing.

$$17$$
$$+\ 66$$

$$\overset{3}{3}9$$
$$+\ 54$$
$$\overline{111}$$

Did I add correctly this time?

4. Add. Make a proof drawing.

$$39$$
$$+\ 54$$

▶ Choose a Method

Add. Use any method.

5. $\begin{array}{r} 73 \\ +\ 42 \\ \end{array}$ $\qquad$ $\begin{array}{r} 26 \\ +\ 85 \\ \end{array}$ $\qquad$ $\begin{array}{r} 58 \\ +\ 34 \\ \end{array}$

© Houghton Mifflin Harcourt Publishing Company

Choose an Addition Method

Cut along the dashed lines.

Dollar Bills

Name _____

▶ **Find the Amount**

Write the answer using ¢.
Then write the answer using $.

Show your work.

1. Joe has 11 dimes and 4 pennies. How
   much money does Joe have?

   _____   _____

2. Bekah has one dollar, 3 dimes, and 8 pennies.
   How much money does Bekah have?

   _____   _____

3. Tim has 14 dimes and 15 pennies. How
   much money does Tim have?

   _____   _____

4. Dinah has 2 dimes, 6 pennies, and 1 dollar.
   How much money does Dinah have?

   _____   _____

5. Lou has 1 dollar, 8 dimes, and 19 pennies.
   How much money does Lou have?

   _____   _____

▶ **The Farm Stand**

Potatoes 65¢	Corn 56¢	Bananas 89¢	Peaches 77¢
Radishes 76¢	Lemons 88¢	Celery 57¢	Peppers 78¢
Mushrooms 67¢	Carrots 86¢	Tomatoes 97¢	Grapes 98¢
Watermelon 59¢	Oranges 85¢	Raspberries 99¢	Green Beans 87¢

► Practice Counting by 5s

1. Go across. Loop groups of 5 bags. Write the numbers.

► How Many Cents?

Under the coins, write the total amount of money so far.
Then write the total using $. The first one is done for you.

2.   5¢   5¢   5¢

   5¢   10¢   15¢ $ _0_ . _1_ _5_

                                              total

3.   5¢   5¢   5¢   5¢

_____   _____   _____   _____ $ __ . __ __

                                              total

4.   5¢   5¢   5¢   5¢   5¢

_____   _____   _____   _____   _____ $ __ . __ __

                                              total

5. Pedro has 9 nickels. Draw s.

Write the total amount of money. $ __ . __ __

                                              total

Name _____

► Nickels and Pennies

Under the coins, write the total amount of money so far.
Then write the total using $. The first one is done for you.

6.   5¢   5¢   1¢

   _5¢_   _10¢_   _11¢_ $ _0_ . _1_ _1_
                                                       total

7.   5¢   5¢   1¢   1¢   1¢

   ____   ____   ____   ____   ____ $ __ . __ __
                                                       total

8.   5¢   5¢   5¢   1¢   1¢

   ____   ____   ____   ____   ____ $ __ . __ __
                                                       total

9. Maneka has 3 nickels and 6 pennies.

   Draw the (5)s and (1)s.

   Write the total amount of money. $ __ . __ __
                                                       total

▶ Dimes, Nickels, and Pennies

Under the coins, write the total amount of money so far.
Then write the total using $. The first one is done for you.

10.   10¢   5¢   1¢

   __10¢__   __15¢__   __16¢__   **$** _0_ . _1_ _6_
                                                     total

11.   10¢   5¢   5¢   1¢   1¢

   _____ _____ _____ _____ _____   **$** __ . __ __
                                                     total

12.   10¢   10¢   10¢   10¢   5¢   1¢

   _____ _____ _____ _____ _____ _____   **$** __ . __ __
                                                     total

13. Cathy has 3 dimes, 4 nickels, and 2 pennies.

Draw s, s, and (1)s.

Write the total amount of money.   **$** __ . __ __
                                                     total

Name _____

► PATH to FLUENCY **Add Within 100**

Add.

1. 36
   + 15
   ____

2. 64
   + 23
   ____

3. 13
   + 22
   ____

4. 47
   + 46
   ____

5. 60
   + 18
   ____

6. 11
   + 63
   ____

7. 28
   + 39
   ____

8. 76
   + 23
   ____

9. 33
   + 58
   ____

10. 63
   + 32
   ____

11. 44
   + 27
   ____

12. 45
   + 54
   ____

► (PATH to FLUENCY) **Add Within 100 (continued)**

Add.

13. 49
   + 51

14. 58
   + 26

15. 12
   + 85

16. 28
   + 31

17. 65
   + 16

18. 42
   + 26

19. 77
   + 19

20. 27
   + 53

21. 35
   + 40

22. 33
   + 67

23. 24
   + 19

24. 82
   + 7

Fluency: Addition Within 100

▶ PATH to FLUENCY **New Ten Challenge**

Work in 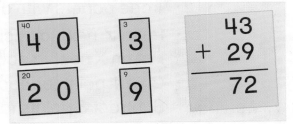. Lay out Secret Code Cards like this.

10	60		1	6
1 0	**6 0**		**1**	**6**
20	70		2	7
2 0	**7 0**		**2**	**7**
30	80		3	8
3 0	**8 0**		**3**	**8**
40	90		4	9
4 0	**9 0**		**4**	**9**
50			5	
5 0			**5**	

1. 🧑 Use Secret Code Cards to help you make a 2-digit addition (sum less than 100).

40	3	43
4 0	**3**	**+ 29**
20	9	
2 0	**9**	**72**

2️⃣ Make another 2-digit addition.

• Use the same tens cards.

• If 🧑 *made a new ten,* use ones cards that *do not make a new ten.*

• If 🧑 *did not make a new ten,* use ones cards that *make a new ten.*

40	3	43
4 0	**3**	**+ 25**
20	5	
2 0	**5**	**68**

Activity continues on next page.

► (PATH to FLUENCY) **New Ten Challenge** (continued)

2. 👥 Work together to check your work.
Correct any errors.

3. Put the Secret Code Cards back. Switch roles and
repeat. Continue until time is up.

*To play as a game and compete with another pair,
use the* **Scoring Rules** *below.*

**Scoring Rules
for
*New Ten Challenge***

· Trade papers with another pair.

· Put a ✓ next to each correct answer.
Put an X next to each incorrect answer.

· Give 1 point for each ✓.
Subtract 3 points for each X.

· The pair with more points wins.

Fluency: Addition Within 100

Name _____

▶ **Practice Adding Three Addends**

Add.

1. $15 + 29 + 36 =$ _____

2. $24 + 27 + 34 =$ _____

3. $36 + 33 + 39 =$ _____

4. $35 + 26 + 17 =$ _____

▶ Practice Adding Four Addends

Add.

5. $18 + 23 + 34 + 17 = $ _____

6. $38 + 32 + 14 + 25 = $ _____

7. $20 + 16 + 33 + 27 = $ _____

8. $26 + 41 + 35 + 12 = $ _____

▶ Math and Recycling

To recycle means to use again. The second graders
at Center School are collecting trash. They will
recycle the trash to make musical instruments.

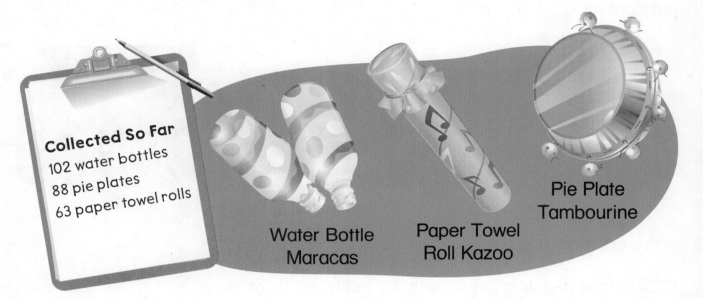

Collected So Far
102 water bottles
88 pie plates
63 paper towel rolls

Water Bottle
Maracas

Paper Towel
Roll Kazoo

Pie Plate
Tambourine

Solve each word problem.

1. Forty-eight children each want to make a pie
   plate tambourine. Each tambourine is made with
   2 pie plates. Do they have enough pie plates?

   Circle yes or no.   yes   no

2. If they collect 10 more water bottles, how many
   water bottles will they have?

   _____
   label

3. If they collect 29 more paper towel rolls, will they
   have enough to make 75 kazoos?

   Circle yes or no.   yes   no

▶ Money for Cans and Bottles

Some states help people recycle by giving money back when they return a bottle or can. This fleece jacket, this yo-yo, and this park bench are all made from recycled plastic bottles.

Solve each word problem.

4. Suzanne and Jing get 5 cents for each can or bottle they return. Suzanne returns 29 cans and 18 bottles. Jing returns 15 cans and 34 bottles. Who gets more money back?

   _____

5. Malia returns 12 bottles. She gets one nickel for each bottle. How much money does she get?

   _____

6. Roberto gets 5 cents for every can he returns. He gets $1.20. How many cans does he return?

   ☐ _____
   label

Draw each number using hundred boxes, ten sticks,
and circles. Then write the number in expanded form.

1. 148

2. 163

_____

_____

What number is shown?

Write the number and the number name.

3. ☐ ‖ ∘∘∘∘

4. ☐ ∘∘∘

_____

_____

_____

_____

Add.

5. 83 + 1 = _____

6. 80 + 10 = _____

7. 60 + 40 = _____

8. 100 + 7 = _____

Compare. Write >, <, or =.

9. 35 ◯ 124

10. 126 ◯ 126

11. 178 ◯ 139

Name _____

Add.

12.   75
    + 24
    ‾‾‾‾

13.   86
    + 32
    ‾‾‾‾

14.   59
    + 37
    ‾‾‾‾

15.   78
    + 95
    ‾‾‾‾

16. 34 + 29 + 75 = _____

17. 27 + 48 + 11 + 15 = _____

Name _____

18. Skip count by 5s.

<u>15</u>   ____   ____   ____   ____   <u>45</u>

Under the coins, write the total amount of money so far.

19.   5¢   5¢   5¢   5¢   1¢   1¢   1¢

<u>5¢</u>   <u>10¢</u>   ____   ____   ____   ____   ____

20.   10¢   10¢   5¢   5¢   5¢   5¢   1¢

<u>10¢</u>   <u>20¢</u>   ____   ____   ____   ____   ____

Solve each word problem.   **Show your work.**

21. Ned has 2 dimes, 3 nickels, and 2 pennies.
How much money does Ned have?
Use ¢ in your answer.

_____

22. Milan has 1 dollar, 2 dimes, and 6 pennies.
How much money does Milan have?
Use $ in your answer.

_____

Solve each word problem.   **Show your work.**

23. Arnez and Jada count insects in the
park. Arnez counts 56 ants. Jada
counts 37 ladybugs. How many insects
do they count altogether?

   [   ] _____
              label

24. Terrel scored 88 points in a computer
game. He scored 43 points in the next
game. How many points did he score
altogether?

   [   ] _____
              label

25. **Extended Response** Explain how you find the sum of
29 and 84. Then make a proof drawing.

_____

_____

_____

_____

Dear Family:

Your child is working on a geometry and measurement unit. In this unit, children will use centimeter rulers to measure line segments and draw shapes.

You can help your child link geometry concepts learned in school with the real world. Encourage your child to find examples of different shapes (triangles, quadrilaterals including rectangles and squares, pentagons, and hexagons) in your home or neighborhood. This will help your child enjoy and understand geometry.

In Lesson 1 of this unit, your child will be asked to find the partner lengths of a line segment. An example is shown below.

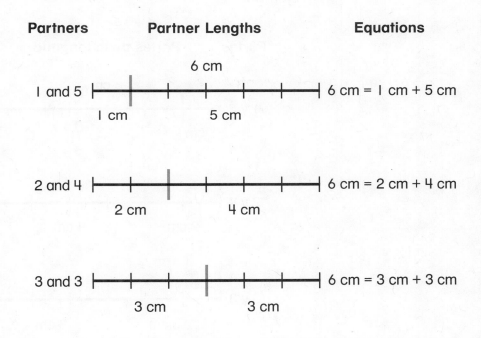

Partners	Partner Lengths	Equations

1 and 5   6 cm   1 cm   5 cm   6 cm = 1 cm + 5 cm

2 and 4   2 cm   4 cm   6 cm = 2 cm + 4 cm

3 and 3   3 cm   3 cm   6 cm = 3 cm + 3 cm

If you have any questions or comments, please call or write to me. Thank you.

Sincerely,
Your child's teacher

COMMON CORE

Unit 3 includes the Common Core Standards for Mathematical Content for Operations and Algebraic Thinking 2.OA.2, Number and Operations in Base Ten 2.NBT.4, 2.NBT.5, 2.NBT.6, Geometry 2.G.1, Measurement and Data 2.MD.1, 2.MD.2, 2.MD.3, 2.MD.4, 2.MD.9, and all Mathematical Practices.

Estimada familia:

Su niño está trabajando en una unidad que trata sobre geometría y medidas. En esta unidad los niños usarán reglas en centímetros para medir segmentos y trazar figuras.

Usted puede ayudar a su niño a relacionar los conceptos de geometría que aprenda en la escuela con el mundo real. Anímelo a buscar ejemplos de diferentes figuras (triángulos, cuadriláteros incluyendo rectángulos y cuadrados, pentágonos y hexágonos), en su casa o en el vecindario. Esto ayudará a su niño a disfrutar y a comprender la geometría.

En la Lección 1 de esta unidad se le pedirá a su niño que halle las partes de la longitud de un segmento. Abajo se muestra un ejemplo.

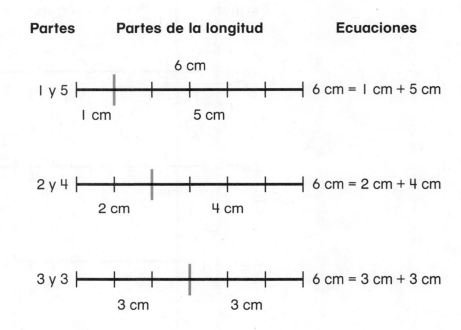

Si tiene alguna pregunta o algún comentario, por favor comuníquese conmigo. Gracias.

Atentamente,
El maestro de su niño

COMMON CORE La Unidad 3 incluye los Common Core Standards for Mathematical Content for Operations and Algebraic Thinking 2.OA.2, Number and Operations in Base Ten 2.NBT.4, 2.NBT.5, 2.NBT.6, Geometry 2.G.1, Measurement and Data 2.MD.1, 2.MD.2, 2.MD.3, 2.MD.4, 2.MD.9, and all Mathematical Practices.

► Count Centimeter Lengths

A **centimeter** is a unit of measure for **length**.
The short way to write centimeters is cm.

|—————|
I cm

You can make a 6-cm **line segment** by pushing together six I-cm line lengths.

You can mark the I-cm lengths.

To find the measure of the line segment, count the I-cm lengths.

Use a centimeter ruler to mark the I-cm lengths.
Count the I-cm lengths.

I. —————————————— [ ] cm

2. ———————————————————————— [ ] cm

3. —————————————————————— [ ] cm

4. —————————————————————————— [ ] cm

VOCABULARY
line segment
horizontal
vertical

▶ Draw Line Segments

You can use a ruler to draw a **line segment** 7 cm long.
Begin drawing at the zero edge of your ruler. Stop
when you have counted seven 1-cm lengths.

Use your centimeter ruler to draw a **horizontal** line
segment with the length given. Mark off and count
1-cm lengths to check the length.

5. 8 cm

6. 5 cm

7. Draw a **vertical** line segment 3 cm long.
   Mark off and count 1-cm lengths to check the length.

▶ The Ruler as a Group of Lengths

> You can think of a ruler as a group of line segments with different lengths.

8. Copy this group of line segments.

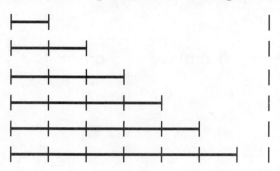

9. Next, draw the same group of line segments closer together.

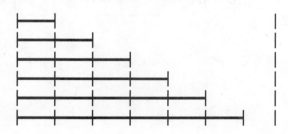

10. Write the number of centimeters at the end of each line segment in Exercise 9.

11. Imagine that you drew the segments so close together that they were on top of each other. What would the segments start to look like?

_____

12. Place a centimeter ruler under your diagram. What do the numbers on the ruler mean?

_____

_____

▶ **Explore Partner Lengths**

13. Show the **partner lengths** for a 6-cm line segment.

Partners	Partner Lengths	Equations

 and ☐   ———————————   6 cm = ☐ cm + ☐ cm

☐ and ☐   ———————————   6 cm = ☐ cm + ☐ cm

☐ and ☐   ———————————   6 cm = ☐ cm + ☐ cm

14. How many different pairs of partner lengths does the 6-cm line segment have?

_____ different pairs

Measure Length

VOCABULARY
square
angle
right angle

► **Draw and Identify Squares**

A **square** is a shape with four equal sides and four **right angles**.

1. Use your centimeter ruler. Draw a square with sides that are each 3 cm long.

Look at these shapes.

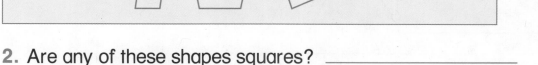

2. Are any of these shapes squares? _____

3. How are the **angles** of these shapes different from the angles of squares?

_____

4. How are the sides of these shapes different from the sides of squares?

_____

5. Is this shape a square? Explain why or why not.

_____

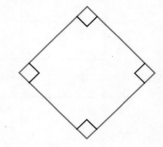

_____

VOCABULARY
rectangle
opposite sides

▶ **Draw and Identify Rectangles**

A **rectangle** is a shape with **opposite sides** that are equal in length and four right angles.

6. Use your centimeter ruler to draw a rectangle that is 6 cm long and 3 cm wide.

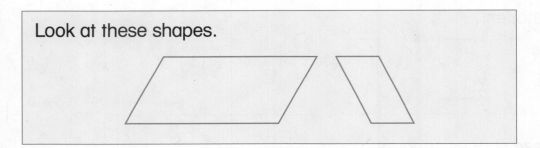

Look at these shapes.

7. Are these shapes rectangles? Explain why or why not.

_____

_____

8. Is a square a rectangle? Explain why or why not.

_____

_____

_____

VOCABULARY
triangle

▶ **Compare Lengths of Sides of Triangles**

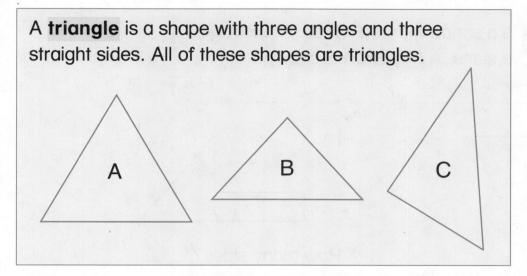

A **triangle** is a shape with three angles and three straight sides. All of these shapes are triangles.

A   B   C

9. Measure each side of Triangle A. What did you discover about the sides?

_____

_____

10. Measure each side of Triangle B. What did you discover about the sides?

_____

_____

11. Measure each side of Triangle C. What did you discover about the sides?

_____

_____

12. Draw a loop to show how much longer the longest side of Triangle C is than the shortest side. The longest side of Triangle C is ☐ cm longer than its shortest side.

VOCABULARY
quadrilateral
pentagon
hexagon

► **Describe Shapes**

A **quadrilateral** is a shape with four sides. A **pentagon** is a shape with five sides. A **hexagon** is a shape with six sides.

13.

How many sides? _____

How many angles? _____

Loop the shape.

quadrilateral

square

hexagon

14.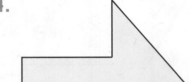

How many sides? _____

How many angles? _____

Loop the shape.

quadrilateral

pentagon

triangle

15.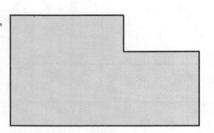

How many sides? _____

How many angles? _____

Loop the shape.

hexagon

triangle

rectangle

16.

How many sides? _____

How many angles? _____

Loop the shape.

rectangle

pentagon

quadrilateral

Recognize and Draw Shapes

► Estimate and Measure Around a Square

Find the distance around each square.

1.

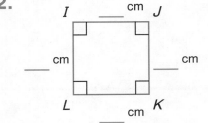

A

cm

cm

B

D

cm

C

cm

____ cm + ____ cm + ____ cm + ____ cm

= ____ cm

2.

I   cm   J

cm   cm

L   cm   K

____ cm + ____ cm + ____ cm + ____ cm

= ____ cm

Estimate and then measure each side.

Then find the distance around the square.

3. a. Complete the table. Use a
        centimeter ruler to measure.

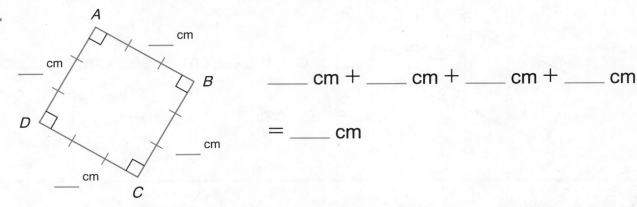

Side	Estimate	Measure
EF		
FG		
GH		
HE		

E   cm   F

cm   cm

H   cm   G

b. Find the distance around the square.

____ cm + ____ cm + ____ cm + ____ cm = ____ cm

Name _____

► **Estimate and Measure Around a Rectangle**

Find the distance around each rectangle.

4.

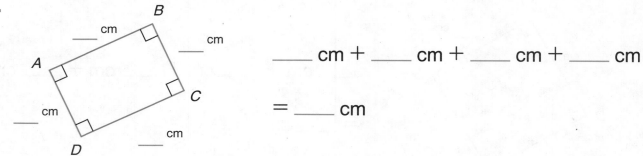

____ cm + ____ cm + ____ cm + ____ cm

= ____ cm

5.

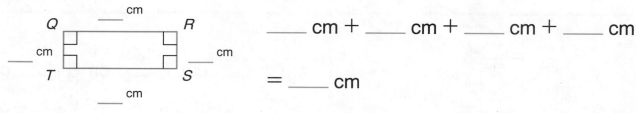

____ cm + ____ cm + ____ cm + ____ cm

= ____ cm

Estimate and then measure each side.

Then find the distance around the rectangle.

6. a. Complete the table. Use a
centimeter ruler to measure.

Side	Estimate	Measure
WX		
XY		
YZ		
ZW		

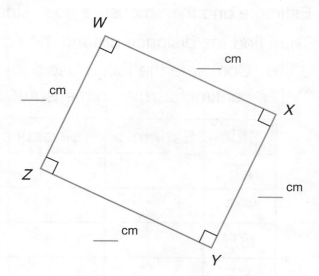

b. Find the distance around the rectangle.

____ cm + ____ cm + ____ cm + ____ cm = ____ cm

Estimate and Measure

Name _____

▶ Estimate and Measure

Find the distance around each triangle.

1.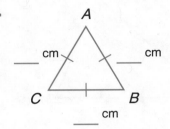

2.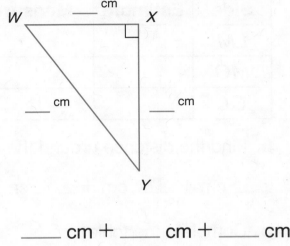

___ cm + ___ cm + ___ cm

= ___ cm

___ cm + ___ cm + ___ cm

= ___ cm

Estimate and then measure each side.

Then find the distance around the triangle.

3. a. Complete the table.

Side	Estimate	Measure
HI		
IJ		
JH		

b. Find the distance around the triangle.

___ cm + ___ cm + ___ cm = ___ cm

► Estimate and Measure (continued)

4. **a.** Complete the table.

Side	Estimate	Measure
LM		
MO		
OL		

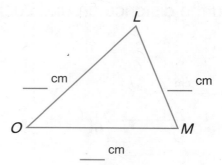

b. Find the distance around the triangle.

____ cm + ____ cm + ____ cm = ____ cm

5. **a.** Complete the table.

Side	Estimate	Measure
DE		
EF		
FD		

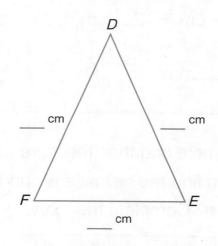

b. Find the distance around the triangle.

____ cm + ____ cm + ____ cm = ____ cm

6. **a.** Complete the table.

Side	Estimate	Measure
PQ		
QR		
RP		

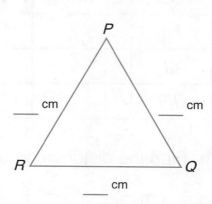

b. Find the distance around the triangle.

____ cm + ____ cm + ____ cm = ____ cm

Name _____

► Rectangular Prisms

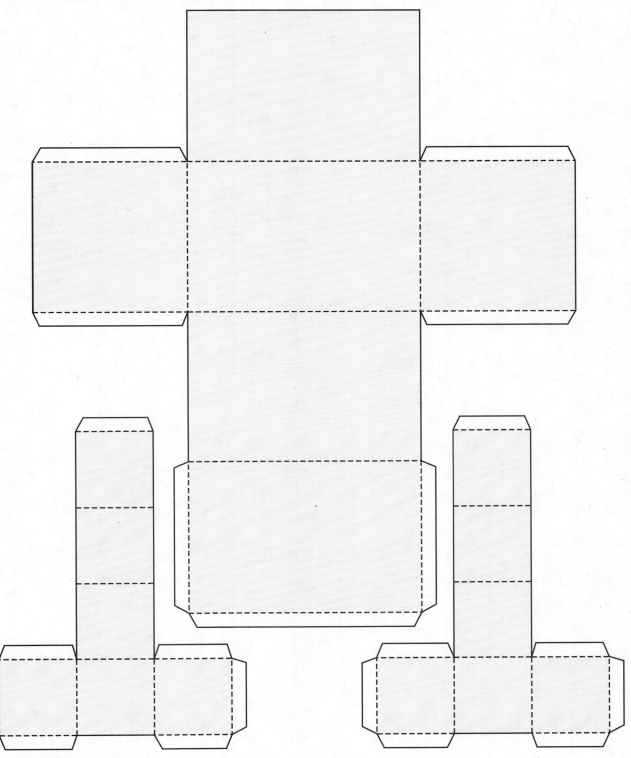

Cut on solid lines.
Fold on dashed lines.

Rectangular Prisms

Name _____

VOCABULARY
rectangular prism
views

▶ Build and Draw Rectangular Prisms

Using unit cubes, build a **rectangular prism** to match each description. Draw the rectangular prism from the top, front, and side **views**.

1. two rows of three unit cubes.

      top view   **front view**   **side view**

2. one row of two unit cubes stacked on top of another row of two unit cubes.

      top view   **front view**   **side view**

▶ Build Rectangular Prisms from Drawings

Build a rectangular prism to match each set of views.

3.   **top view**   **front view**   **side view**

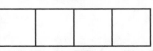

4.   **top view**   **front view**   **side view**

▶ Identify Shapes

A	B	C
D	E	F
G	H	I
J	K	L

Family Letter

Dear Family:

In this unit, your child will be collecting measurement data and using that data to make line plots. A *line plot* is a display that uses a number line and dots (or other marks) to represent data. For this reason, line plots are sometimes called *dot plots*.

Your child will be asked to bring one or two pencils to school. The length of each pencil should be more than 1 inch and less than 8 inches. Children will work in small groups. They will measure each pencil brought in by the members of their group and then make a line plot similar to the one shown below.

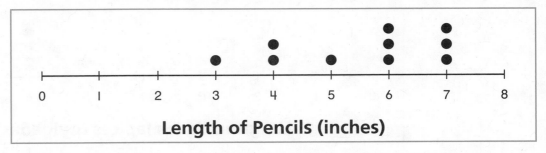

Length of Pencils (inches)

In this unit, your child will also be given several experiences that will help build understanding that the smaller the unit used to measure a given length or distance, the more of those units will be needed.

So, for example, since centimeters are shorter than inches, when the paintbrush below is measured in both centimeters and inches, the number of centimeters is more than the number of inches.

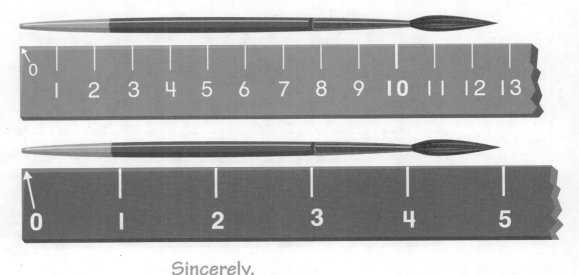

Sincerely,

Your child's teacher

© Houghton Mifflin Harcourt Publishing Company

Unit 3 includes the Common Core Standards for Mathematical Content for Operations and Algebraic Thinking 2.OA.2, Numbers and Operations in Base Ten 2.NBT.4, 2.NBT.5, 2.NBT.6, Geometry 2.G.1, Measurement and Data 2.MD.1, 2.MD.2, 2.MD.3, 2.MD.4, 2.MD.9, and all Mathematical Practices.

Estimada familia:

En esta unidad, su niño reunirá datos sobre medidas y usará esos datos para hacer diagramas de puntos. Un *diagrama de puntos* es un diagrama que usa una recta numérica y puntos u otras marcas para representar datos.

Se le pedirá a su niño que traiga uno o dos lápices a la escuela. Cada lápiz debe medir más de 1 pulgada de longitud pero menos de 8. Los niños trabajarán en grupos pequeños. Medirán los lápices de cada miembro de su grupo y luego, harán un diagrama de puntos como el que se muestra debajo.

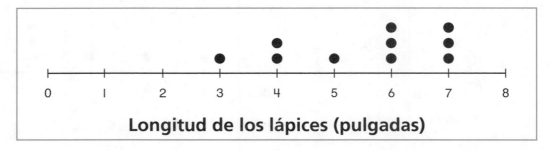

Longitud de los lápices (pulgadas)

También en esta unidad, a su niño se le brindarán diversas experiencias que lo ayudarán a comprender que entre más pequeña sea la unidad que se use para medir una determinada longitud o distancia, más de esas unidades se necesitarán.

Entonces, por ejemplo, como los centímetros son más cortos que las pulgadas, cuando el pincel de abajo se mide en centímetros y en pulgadas, el número de centímetros es mayor que el número de pulgadas.

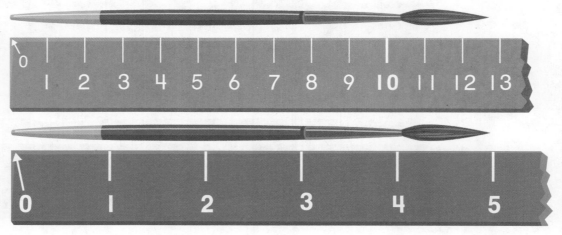

Atentamente,
El maestro de su niño

La Unidad 3 incluye los Common Core Standards for Mathematical Content for Operations and Algebraic Thinking 2.OA.2, Numbers and Operations in Base Ten 2.NBT.4, 2.NBT.5, 2.NBT.6, Geometry 2.G.1, Measurement and Data 2.MD.1, 2.MD.2, 2.MD.3, 2.MD.4, 2.MD.9, and all Mathematical Practices.

Estimate and Measure with Centimeters

25 ↑	50 ↑	75 ↑	100 ↑
24	49	74	99
23	48	73	98
22	47	72	97
21	46	71	96
20	45	70	95
19	44	69	94
18	43	68	93
17	42	67	92
16	41	66	91
15	40	65	90
14	39	64	89
13	38	63	88
12	37	62	87
11	36	61	86
10	35	60	85
9	34	59	84
8	33	58	83
7	32	57	82
6	31	56	81
5	30	55	80
4	29	54	79
3	28	53	78
2	27	52	77
1	26	51	76
	25 ↓	50 ↓	75 ↓

Side labels: 50, 20, 40, 10, 30 (left column); 100, 70, 90, 60, 80 (right columns)

Step 1: Cut out on the dashed lines.

Step 2: Put the sections in order.

Step 3: Tape or paste the sections together.

← 100

← 76
← 74   Tape or paste

← 51   Tape or paste
← 49

← 26   Tape or paste
← 24

← 1

► **Estimate and Measure**

Find a part of your hand that is about each length.

1. 1 cm _____

2. 10 cm _____

Find a part of your body that is about 1 meter long.

3. 1 m _____

Find the real object. Estimate and measure its length.
Choose the nearest centimeter endpoint.

4.

Estimate: about _____ cm

Measure: _____ cm

5.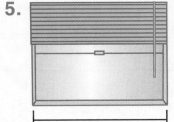

Estimate: about _____ cm

Measure: _____ cm

6.

Estimate: about _____ cm

Measure: _____ cm

7.

Estimate: about _____ m

Measure: _____ m

Draw a line segment to show each length.

8. 1 cm

9. 10 cm

▶ Measure Heights

When you measure a length greater than 1 meter, you place two meter sticks end to end. The first meter stick is 100 cm. You add 100 to the number of centimeters you read from the second meter stick.

10. Complete the table for each person in your group.

Person's Name	Estimated Height (cm)	Actual Height (cm)	Difference Between Estimated and Actual Height (cm)

Use the table you collected to answer these questions.

11. Who is the tallest person in your group?

_____

12. How much taller is the tallest person than the shortest person? Measure this difference and check by adding. _____

13. Whose estimated height was closest to his or her actual height? _____

14. On a separate sheet of paper, use the table to write four more questions. Trade your questions with another group and answer each other's questions.

▶ Introduce Line Plots

Look at this **line plot**.

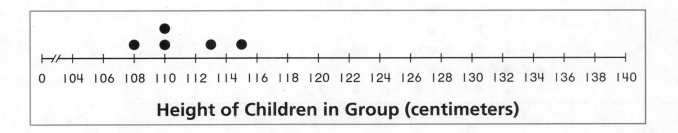

Height of Children in Group (centimeters)

▶ Make a Line Plot

15. Draw dots for the heights of the children in your group. Use data from the table on page 138.

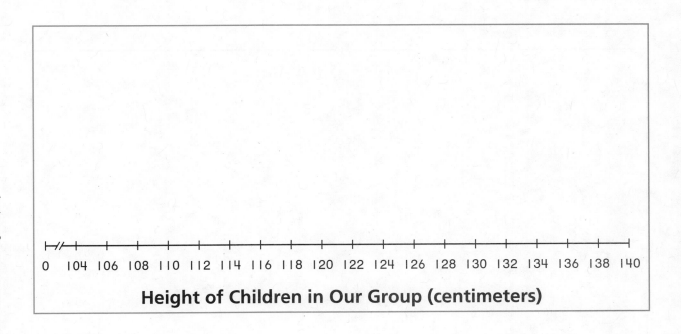

Height of Children in Our Group (centimeters)

▶ Discuss a Line Plot

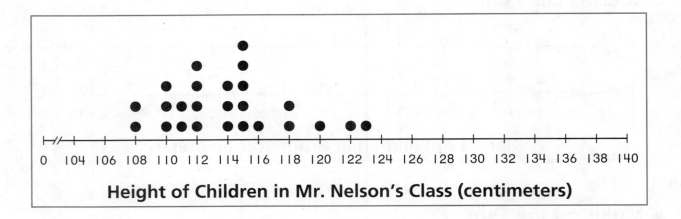

Height of Children in Mr. Nelson's Class (centimeters)

▶ Show Class Data on a Line Plot

16. Draw dots for the heights of the children in your class.

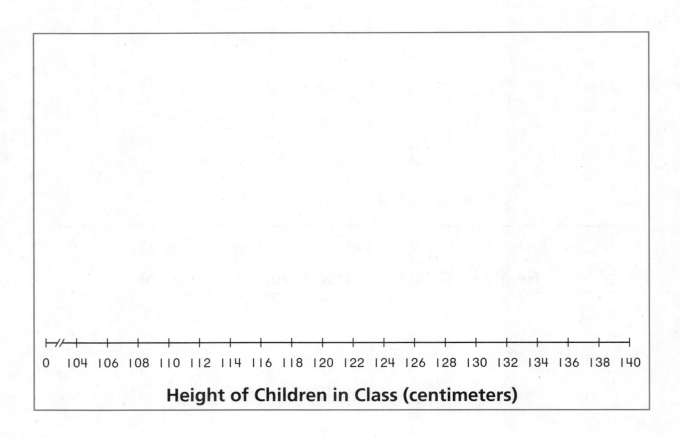

Height of Children in Class (centimeters)

▶ Make an Inch Ruler

Directions:

Step 1: Cut along the dashed lines.

Step 2: Place the sections in the correct order.

Step 3: Tape or glue together the sections at the tab.

Step 4: Write a **6** where the two strips meet.

TAB

— 5

— 4

— 3

— 2

— 1

— 0

— 12

— 11

— 10

— 9

— 8

— 7

TAB

— 5

— 4

— 3

— 2

— 1

— 0

— 12

— 11

— 10

— 9

— 8

— 7

Inch Ruler

► **Measure to the Nearest Inch**

To measure to the nearest **inch (in.)**, place the zero mark on your ruler at the left end of the object. Find the inch mark that is closest to the right end of the object.

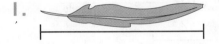

To the nearest inch, the length of this toy car is 2 inches.
Measure the length of each object to the nearest inch.

1. 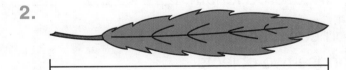 _____

2.  _____

3. _____

4. Draw a horizontal line segment that is 2 in. long.

5. Draw a horizontal line segment that is 6 in. long.

▶ Estimate and Measure in Inches

6. Describe a part of your hand that measures about 2 in.

   _____

7. Describe a part of your hand that measures about 1 in.

   _____

8. Describe a part of your hand that measures about 6 in.

   _____

Estimate and measure the length of each line segment.

9. ├──────────────────────────────┤

   Estimated length: _____   Measured length: _____

10. ├──┤

    Estimated length: _____   Measured length: _____

11. Find four classroom objects that you can measure in
    inches and then in centimeters. Choose two objects
    with a length between 12 inches and 24 inches.
    Complete the table.

Object	Estimated length (in.)	Measured length (in.)	Measured length (cm)

► Make a Yardstick

Directions:

Step 1: Cut along the dashed lines.

Step 2: Place the sections in the correct order.

Step 3: Tape or glue together the sections at the tab.

TAB	TAB	TAB	TAB	TAB	
	1 ft		2 ft		36 3 ft
5	11	17	23	29	35
4	10	16	22	28	34
3	9	15	21	27	33
2	8	14	20	26	32
1	7	13	19	25	31
0	6		18		30

VOCABULARY
foot (ft)
yard (yd)

▶ Measure in Feet and Yards

Find each length to the nearest **foot (ft)**.

12. width of your desk

13. length from your knee to your ankle

_____

_____

Find each length to the nearest **yard (yd).**

14. height of the classroom door

15. length of a bookshelf

_____

_____

Measure each length to the nearest foot and to the nearest yard.

16. width of the classroom door

17. length of the classroom board

_____ ft

_____ ft

_____ yd

_____ yd

18. What do you notice about the numbers when you measure in yards instead of feet? Why?

_____

_____

▶ Estimate and Measure Height

Estimate your height in inches. Then work with a partner to find your actual height.

19. Estimate: _____

20. Actual height: _____

▶ Height in Centimeters and Inches

Draw a dot to show your height in centimeters.

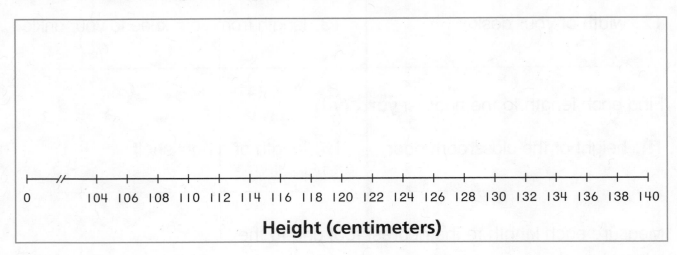

Height (centimeters)

Draw a dot to show your height in inches.

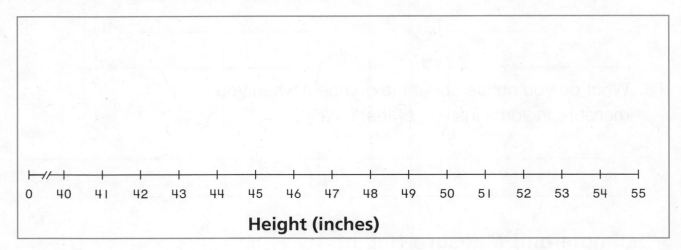

Height (inches)

Estimate and Measure with Inches

▶ **Lengths of Pencils**

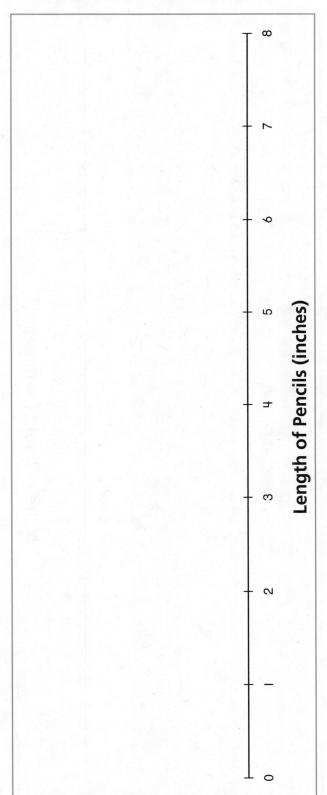

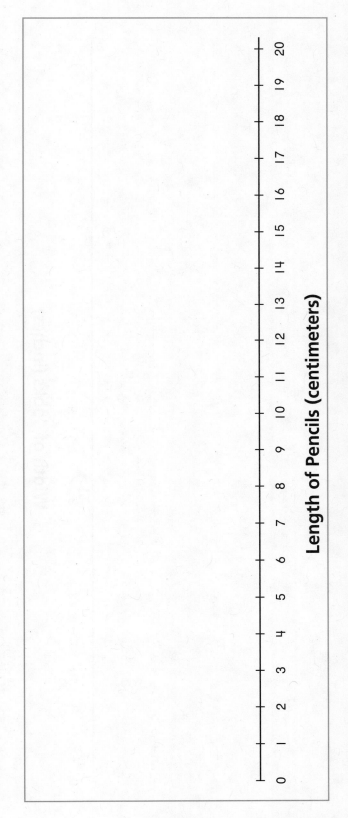

► **Width of Books**

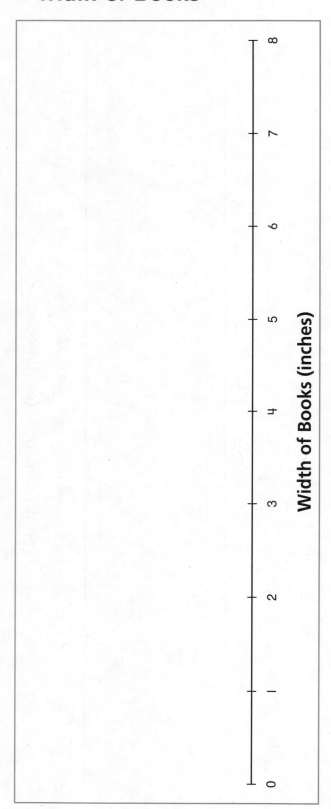

Width of Books (inches)

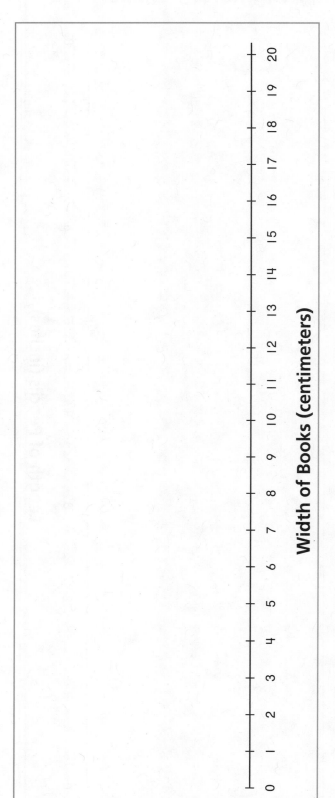

Width of Books (centimeters)

►Measurement Data on Line Plots

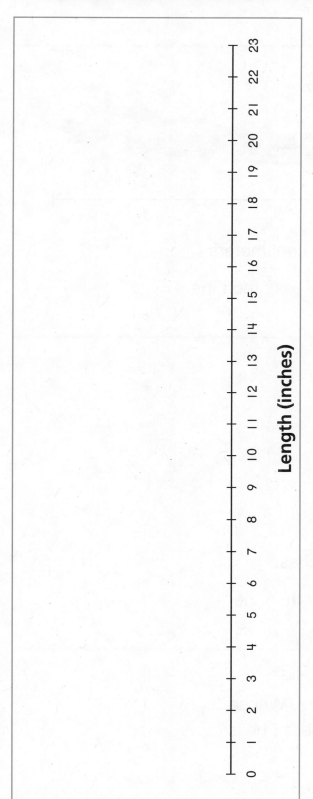

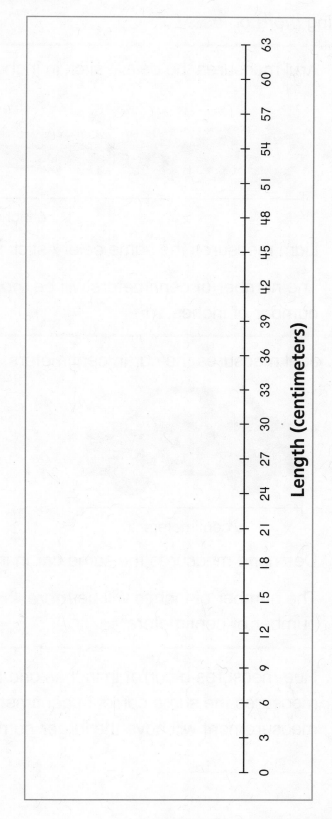

► **Compare Measurement Units**

Ring *more* or *less*.

1. Arul measures the celery stick in inches.

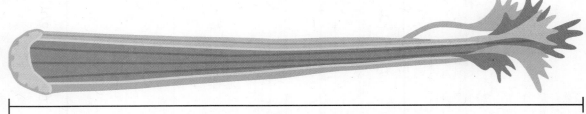

6 inches

Liam measures the same celery stick in centimeters.

The number of centimeters will be *more* *less* than the number of inches.

2. Jael measures the car in centimeters.

6 centimeters

Desmond measures the same car in inches.

The number of inches will be *more* *less* than the number of centimeters.

3. Rue measures a carrot in inches and Peter measures the same carrot in centimeters. Whose measurement will have the larger number of units?

_____

▶ Math and Quilts

A patchwork quilt is made by sewing pieces of cloth together. Look for shapes in these patchwork quilts.

1. Color each shape a different color.

Shape	triangle	quadrilateral	pentagon	hexagon
Color	red	orange	blue	yellow

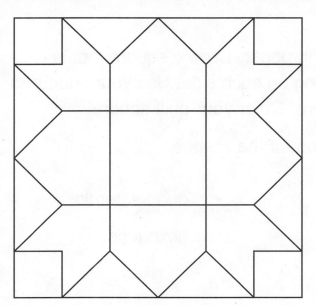

Name _____

► Make Quilts

2. Continue the pattern to complete this quilt square.

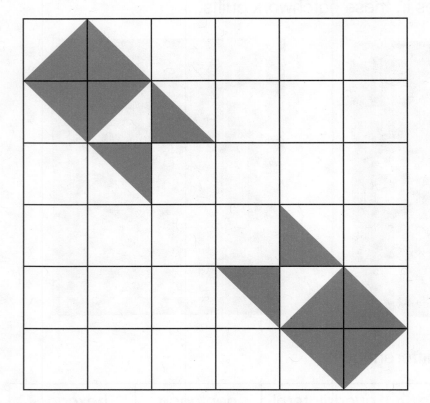

3. Use centimeter grid paper. Draw a square that is 16 centimeters long on each side. Use your square to make a quilt pattern. Color your quilt square.

When you finish, count the shapes.

_____ triangles   _____ quadrilaterals

_____ pentagons   _____ hexagons

Name _____

Measure each string to the nearest centimeter.

1. [ ] cm

2. [ ] cm

3. [ ] cm

4. [ ] cm

5. [ ] cm

6. [ ] cm

7. Show the lengths of the strings on this line plot.

```
|----|----|----|----|----|----|----|----|
0    1    2    3    4    5    6    7    8
```

Lengths of Strings (centimeters)

8. Estimate and then measure the paintbrush in inches.

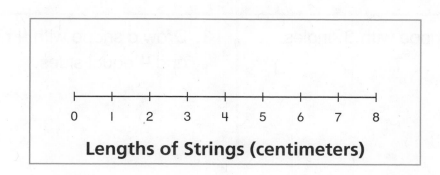

Estimate

[ ] inches

Measure

[ ] inches

9. Draw a loop and then measure to find how much longer the blue pencil is than the yellow pencil.

The blue pencil is _____ inches longer than the yellow pencil.

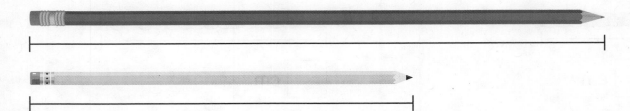

10. Draw a shape with 5 angles.	11. Draw a shape with 6 sides.
12. Draw a shape with 3 angles.	13. Draw a shape with 4 right angles and 4 equal sides.

14. Draw a shape with 6 equal faces.

Name each shape. Choose a word from the box.

cube	hexagon	triangle
pentagon		quadrilateral

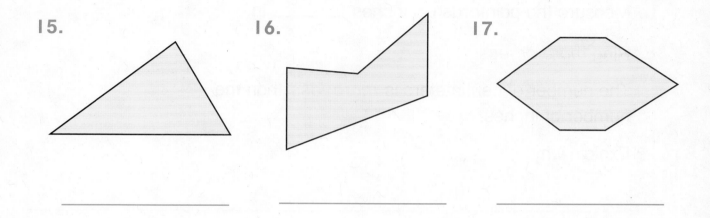

15. _____

16. _____

17. _____

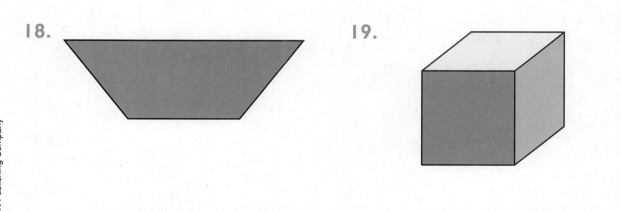

18. _____

19. _____

20. Extended Response

a. Measure the paintbrush in centimeters. _____ cm

b. Measure the paintbrush in inches. _____ in.

c. Ring *more* or *less*.

The number of centimeters is *more less* than the number of inches.

Explain why.

_____

_____

_____

Problem Types

	Result Unknown	Change Unknown	Start Unknown
Add To	Aisha has 46 stamps in her collection. Then her grandfather gives her 29 stamps. How many stamps does she have now? *Situation and Solution Equation*[1]: $46 + 29 = \square$	Aisha has 46 stamps in her collection. Then her grandfather gives her some stamps. Now she has 75 stamps. How many stamps did her grandfather give her? *Situation Equation:* $46 + \square = 75$ *Solution Equation:* $\square = 75 - 46$	Aisha has some stamps in her collection. Then her grandfather gives her 29 stamps. Now she has 75 stamps. How many stamps did she have to start? *Situation Equation:* $\square + 29 = 75$ *Solution Equation:* $\square = 75 - 29$
Take From	A store has 43 bottles of water at the start of the day. During the day, the store sells 25 bottles. How many bottles do they have at the end of the day? *Situation and Solution Equation:* $43 - 25 = \square$	A store has 43 bottles of water at the start of the day. The store has 18 bottles left at the end of the day. How many bottles does the store sell? *Situation Equation:* $43 - \square = 18$ *Solution Equation:* $\square = 43 - 18$	A store sells 25 bottles of water during one day. At the end of the day 18 bottles are left. How many bottles did the store have at the beginning of the day? *Situation Equation:* $\square - 25 = 18$ *Solution Equation:* $\square = 25 + 18$

[1] A situation equation represents the structure (action) in the problem situation. A solution equation shows the operation used to find the answer.

Problem Types continued

Problem Types (continued)

	Total Unknown	Addend Unknown	Both Addends Unknown
Put Together/ Take Apart	A clothing store has 39 shirts with short sleeves and 45 shirts with long sleeves. How many shirts does the store have in all? *Math Drawing²:* 39 45 *Situation and Solution Equation:* $39 + 45 = \square$	Of the 84 shirts in a clothing store, 39 have short sleeves. The rest have long sleeves. How many shirts have long sleeves? *Math Drawing:* 84 39 *Situation Equation:* $84 = 39 + \square$ *Solution Equation:* $84 - 39 = \square$	Pam has 24 roses. How many can she put in her red vase and how many in her blue vase? *Math Drawing:* 24 *Situation Equation:* $24 = \square + \square$

²These math drawings are called Math Mountains in Grades 1–3 and break-apart drawings in Grades 4 and 5.

	Difference Unknown	**Greater Unknown**	**Smaller Unknown**
Compare[1]	Alex has 64 trading cards. Lucy has 48 trading cards. How many **more** trading cards does **Alex** have than Lucy? Lucy has 48 trading cards. Alex has 64 trading cards. How many **fewer** trading cards does **Lucy** have than Alex? *Math Drawing:* A $\boxed{64}$ L $\boxed{48}$ $\bigcirc{?}$ *Situation Equation:* $48 + \square = 64$ or $\square = 64 - 48$ *Solution Equation:* $\square = 64 - 48$	**Leading Language** Lucy has 48 trading cards. **Alex** has **16 more** trading cards than Lucy. How many trading cards does Alex have? --- **Misleading Language** Lucy has 48 trading cards. **Lucy** has **16 fewer** trading cards than Alex. How many trading cards does Alex have? *Math Drawing:* A $\boxed{?}$ L $\boxed{48}$ $\bigcirc{16}$ *Situation and Solution Equation:* $48 + 16 = \square$	**Leading Language** Alex has 64 trading cards. **Lucy** has **16 fewer** trading cards than Alex. How many trading cards does Lucy have? --- **Misleading Language** Alex has 64 trading cards. **Alex** has **16 more** trading cards than Lucy. How many trading cards does Lucy have? *Math Drawing:* A $\boxed{64}$ L $\boxed{?}$ $\bigcirc{16}$ *Situation Equation:* $\square + 16 = 64$ or $\square = 64 - 16$ *Solution Equation:* $\square = 64 - 16$

[1]A comparison sentence can always be said in two ways. One way uses *more*, and the other uses *fewer* or *less*. Misleading language suggests the wrong operation. For example, it says *Lucy has 16 fewer trading cards than Alex*, but you have to add 16 cards to the number of cards Lucy has to get the number of cards Alex has.

Glossary

5-groups

|||| |||| tens in 5-groups

OOOOO
OOOOO   ones in 5-groups

A

add

●●●●   ●●

$4 + 2 = 6$

addend

$5 + 6 = 11$

↑   ↑

addends

Adding Up Method (for Subtraction)

$$\begin{array}{r} 144 \\ -\ 68 \\ \hline 76 \end{array}$$

$68 + 2 = 70$
$70 + 30 = 100$
$100 + 44 = 144$

$\boxed{76}$

addition doubles

Both addends (or partners) are the same.

$4 + 4 = 8$

A.M.

Use A.M. for times between midnight and noon.

analog clock

angle

These are angles.

array

This rectangular array has
3 rows and 5 columns.

bar graph

Coins in My Collection

horizontal bar graph

Flowers in My Garden

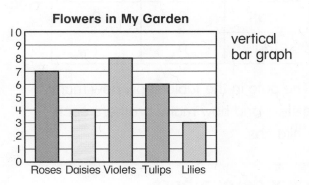

vertical bar graph

break-apart

You can break apart a larger number to get two smaller amounts called break-aparts.

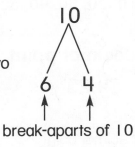

break-aparts of 10

C

cent

front   back

1 cent or 1¢ or $0.01

centimeter (cm)

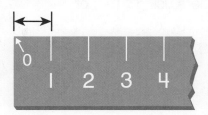

cent sign

56¢

↑

cent sign

clock

analog clock

digital clock

column

This rectangular array has 4 columns with 3 tiles in each column.

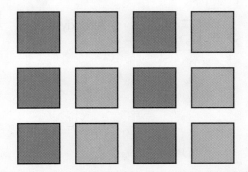

compare numbers

Compare numbers using >, <, or =.

$52 > 25$

$25 < 52$

$25 = 25$

comparison bars

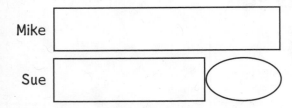

Mike

Sue

You can add labels and fill in numbers to help you solve *Compare* problems.

count all

$5 + 3 = \square$

1 2 3 4 5   6 7 8

• • • • •   • • •

$5 + 3 = \boxed{8}$

count on

$5 + 3 = \boxed{8}$

$5 + \boxed{3} = 8$

$8 - 5 = \boxed{3}$

Already **5**

cube

D

data

	Sisters	Brothers
Kendra	2	1
Scott	2	0
Ida	0	1

data

The data in the table show how many sisters and how many brothers each child has.

decade numbers

10, 20, 30, 40, 50, 60, 70, 80, 90

decimal point

$4.25

decimal point

diagonal

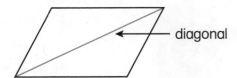

diagonal

difference

$$11 - 3 = 8$$

$$\begin{array}{r} 11 \\ -\ 3 \\ \hline 8 \end{array}$$

difference ⟶ 8

digital clock

digits

0, 1, 2, 3, 4, 5, 6, 7, 8, 9

15 is a 2-digit number.

The 1 in 15 means 1 ten.

The 5 in 15 means 5 ones.

dime

front   back

10 cents or 10¢ or $0.10

dollar

100 cents or

100¢ or $1.00

front

back

dollar sign

$4.25

dollar sign

doubles minus 1

$7 + 7 = 14$, so

$7 + 6 = 13$, 1 less than 14.

doubles minus 2

$7 + 7 = 14$, so

$7 + 5 = 12$, 2 less than 14.

doubles plus 1

$6 + 6 = 12$, so

$6 + 7 = 13$, 1 more than 12.

doubles plus 2

$6 + 6 = 12$, so

$6 + 8 = 14$, 2 more than 12.

E

equal shares

2 halves   4 fourths

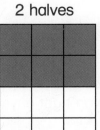 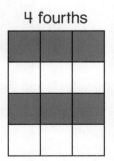

equal to (=)

$$5 + 3 = 8$$

5 plus 3 is equal to 8.

equation

$$4 + 3 = 7 \qquad 7 = 4 + 3$$
$$9 - 5 = 4 \qquad 4 + 5 = 8 + 1$$

An equation must have an $=$ sign.

equation chain

$$3 + 4 = 5 + 2 = 8 - 1 = 7$$

even number

A number is even if you can make groups of 2 and have none left over.

8 is an even number.

exact change

I will pay with 4 dimes and 3 pennies. That is the exact change. I won't get any money back.

expanded form

$$283 = 200 + 80 + 3$$

Expanded Method (for Addition)

$$78 = 70 + 8$$
$$\underline{+\,57} = \underline{50 + 7}$$
$$120 + 15 = 135$$

Expanded Method (for Subtraction)

$$64 = \overset{50}{\cancel{60}} + \overset{14}{\cancel{4}}$$
$$\underline{-\,28} = \underline{20 + 8}$$
$$30 + 6 = 36$$

extra information

Franny has 8 kittens and 2 dogs. 4 kittens are asleep. How many kittens are awake?

$$8 - 4 = \boxed{4}$$

The number of dogs is extra information. It is not needed to solve the problem.

F

fewer

There are fewer ☐ than △.

foot (ft)

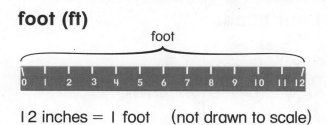

foot

12 inches = 1 foot   (not drawn to scale)

fourth

square

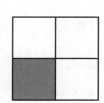

The picture shows 4 fourths. A fourth of the square is shaded.

G

greater than (>)

| |°°°° | |°°°°°

34   >   25

34 is greater than 25.

greatest

25   41   63

63 is the greatest number.

group name

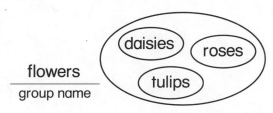

flowers
_____
group name

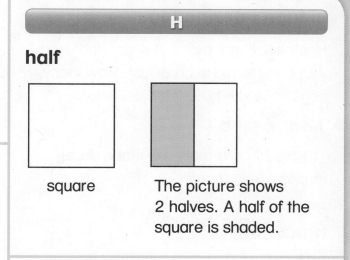

H

half

square

The picture shows 2 halves. A half of the square is shaded.

half hour

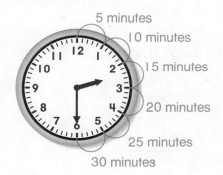

5 minutes
10 minutes
15 minutes
20 minutes
25 minutes
30 minutes

30 minutes = 1 half hour

hexagon

A hexagon has 6 sides and 6 angles.

hidden information

Heather bought a dozen eggs. She used 7 of them to make breakfast. How many eggs does she have left?

$12 - 7 = \boxed{5}$

The hidden information is that a dozen means 12.

horizontal

$4 + 5 = 9$

horizontal form   horizontal line

horizontal bar graph

Coins in My Collection

hour

60 minutes = 1 hour

hour hand

hour hand

hundreds

3 hundreds

347 has 3 hundreds.

hundreds

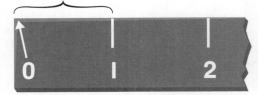

inch (in.)

1 inch

least

14   7   63

7 is the least number.

length

The length of the pencil is about 17 cm.
(not to scale)

less than (<)

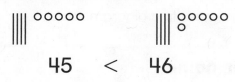

45   <   46

45 is less than 46.

line plot

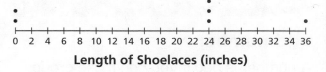

Length of Shoelaces (inches)

line segment

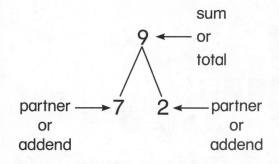

M

make a ten

$8 + 6 = \square$

8 •• | ••••

10 + 4
10 + 4 = 14,
so 8 + 6 = 14

matching drawing

OOO   fewer
OOOOOO   more

Math Mountain

sum
or
total

9

partner   7   2   partner
or   or
addend   addend

meter(m)

100 centimeters = 1 meter
(not drawn to scale)

minus

$8 - 3 = 5$

$$\begin{array}{r} 8 \\ -\ 3 \\ \hline 5 \end{array}$$

8 minus 3 equals 5.

minute

1 minute

60 seconds = 1 minute

Glossary (continued)

minute hand

minute hand: points to the minutes

more

There are more ◯ than ■.

New Groups Above Method

$$\begin{array}{r} {\scriptstyle 1} \\ 56 \\ +\ 28 \\ \hline 84 \end{array}$$

$6 + 8 = 14$
The 1 new ten in 14 goes up to the tens place.

New Groups Below Method

$$\begin{array}{r} 56 \\ +\ 28 \\ \hline {\scriptstyle 1}\ 84 \end{array}$$

$6 + 8 = 14$
The 1 new ten in 14 goes below in the tens place.

nickel

front

back

5 cents or 5¢ or $0.05

not equal to (≠)

$6 + 4 \neq 8$

$6 + 4$ is not equal to 8.

number line diagram

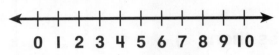

This is a number line diagram.

number name

12

twelve ⟵ number name

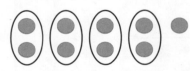

odd number

A number is odd if you can make groups of 2 and have one left over.

9 is an odd number.

ones

7 ones

347 has 7 ones.

↑ ones

© Houghton Mifflin Harcourt Publishing Company

opposite operations

Addition and subtraction are opposite operations.

$$5 + 9 = 14$$
$$14 - 9 = 5$$

Use addition to check subtraction. Use subtraction to check addition.

opposite sides

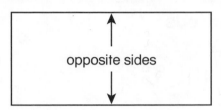

opposite sides

order

2, 5, 6

The numbers 2, 5, and 6 are in order from least to greatest.

P

pair

A group of 2 is a pair.

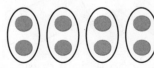

The picture shows 4 pairs of counters.

partner lengths

partner lengths of 4 cm

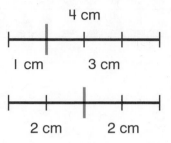

partners

$$9 + 6 = 15$$

partners (addends)

penny

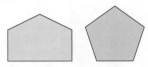

front   back

1 cent or 1¢ or $0.01

pentagon

A pentagon has 5 sides and 5 angles.

Glossary (continued)

picture graph

Flowers	🌼 🌼 🌼 🌼 🌼 🌼	
Vases	🏺 🏺 🏺 🏺 🏺 🏺 🏺 🏺 🏺	

plus

$$3 + 2 = 5$$

3 plus 2 equals 5.

$$\begin{array}{r} 3 \\ + 2 \\ \hline 5 \end{array}$$

P.M.

Use P.M. for times between noon and midnight.

proof drawing

$$86 + 57 = 143$$

Q

quadrilateral

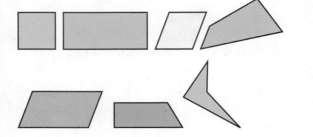

A quadrilateral has 4 sides and 4 angles.

quarter

front   back

25 cents or 25¢ or $0.25
A quarter is another name for a fourth.
A quarter is a fourth of a dollar.

quick hundreds

347

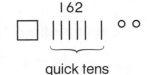

quick hundreds

quick tens

162

□ ||||| | ∘ ∘

quick tens

R

rectangle

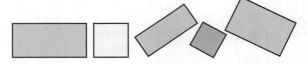

A rectangle has 4 sides and 4 right angles.
Opposite sides have the same length.

rectangular prism

right angle

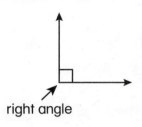

right angle

A right angle is sometimes called a *square corner*.

row

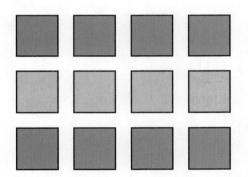

This rectangular array has 3 rows with 4 tiles in each row.

ruler

A ruler is used to measure length.

scale

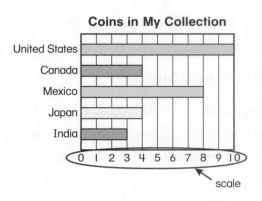

Coins in My Collection

scale

The numbers along the side or the bottom of a graph.

Show All Totals Method

$$
\begin{array}{r}
25 \\
+\,48 \\
\hline
60 \\
13 \\
\hline
73
\end{array}
\qquad
\begin{array}{r}
724 \\
+\,158 \\
\hline
800 \\
70 \\
12 \\
\hline
882
\end{array}
$$

situation equation

A baker baked 100 loaves of bread. He sold some loaves. There are 73 loaves left. How many loaves of bread did he sell?

$100 - \boxed{} = 73$

situation equation

skip count

skip count by 2s: 2, 4, 6, 8, . . .
skip count by 5s: 5, 10, 15, 20, . . .
skip count by 10s: 10, 20, 30, 40, 50, . . .

solution equation

A baker baked 100 loaves of bread. He sold some loaves. There are 73 loaves left. How many loaves of bread did he sell?

$$100 - 73 = \boxed{}$$

solution equation

square

A square has 4 equal sides and 4 right angles.

subtract

$$8 - 5 = 3$$

subtraction doubles

Both addends or partners are the same.
$$8 - 4 = 4$$

sum

$$4 + 3 = 7$$

$$\begin{array}{r} 4 \\ + 3 \\ \hline 7 \end{array}$$

sum $\longrightarrow$

survey

When you collect data by asking people questions, you are taking a survey.

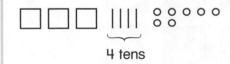

teen number

any number from 11 to 19

11 12 13 14 15 16 17 18 19

tens

4 tens

347 has 4 tens.

tens

third

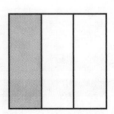

square

The picture shows 3 thirds. A third of the square is shaded.

thousand

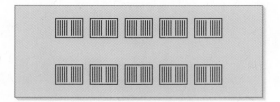

1,000 = ten hundreds

total

10 ←—total
8 2

triangle

A triangle has 3 sides and 3 angles.

U

ungroup

Ungroup when you need more ones or tens to subtract.

Ungroup First Method

$$\begin{array}{r} 6\,4 \\ -2\,8 \\ \hline \end{array}$$
↑ ↑
yes no

$$\begin{array}{r} {}^5\!\!\!\not{6}\,{}^{14}\!\!\not{4} \\ -2\,8 \\ \hline \end{array}$$

$$\begin{array}{r} {}^5\!\!\!\not{6}\,{}^{14}\!\!\not{4} \\ -2\,8 \\ \hline 3\,6 \end{array}$$

1. Check to see if there are enough tens and ones to subtract.

2. You can get more ones by taking from the tens and putting them in the ones place.

3. Subtract from either right to left or left to right.

unknown addend

$$3 + \boxed{} = 9$$
↑
unknown addend

unknown total

$$3 + 6 = \boxed{}$$
↑
unknown total

V

vertical

$$\begin{array}{r} 4 \\ +3 \\ \hline 7 \end{array}$$

vertical form   vertical line

Glossary (continued)

vertical bar graph

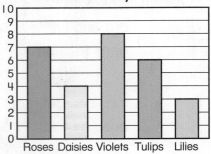

Flowers in My Garden

view

This is the side view of the rectangular prism above.

W

width

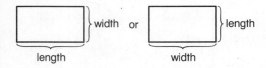

width or length

length   width

Y

yard (yd)

3 feet = 1 yard (not drawn to scale)